THE [REAPPEARANCE]

OF
THE CHRIST

by
ALICE A. BAILEY

LUCIS PUBLISHING COMPANY
New York

LUCIS PRESS, LTD.
London

COPYRIGHT © 1948 BY LUCIS TRUST
COPYRIGHT © RENEWED 1976 BY LUCIS TRUST

First Printing, 1948
Fifth Printing, 1962 (First Paperback Edition)
Twelfth Printing, 2006

ISBN No. 0-85330-114-X
Library of Congress Catalog Card Number: 48-011756

The publication of this book is financed by the Tibetan Book Fund which is established for the perpetuation of the teachings of the Tibetan and Alice A. Bailey.

This Fund is controlled by the Lucis Trust, a tax-exempt, religious, educational corporation.

The Lucis Publishing Company is a non-profit organisation owned by the Lucis Trust. No royalties are paid on this book.

This title is also available
in a clothbound edition.

It has been translated into Bulgarian, Croatian, Danish, Dutch, Finnish, French, German, Greek, Icelandic, Japanese, Polish, Portuguese, Romanian, Russian, Spanish, and Swedish. Translation into other languages is proceeding.

LUCIS PUBLISHING COMPANY
120 Wall Street
New York, NY 10005

LUCIS PRESS, LTD.
Suite 54
3 Whitehall Court
London SW1A 2EF

MANUFACTURED IN THE UNITED STATES OF AMERICA

BOOKS BY ALICE A. BAILEY

Initiation, Human and Solar
Letters on Occult Meditation
The Consciousness of the Atom
A Treatise on Cosmic Fire
The Light of the Soul
The Soul and Its Mechanism
From Intellect to Intuition
A Treatise on White Magic
From Bethlehem to Calvary
Discipleship in the New Age — Vol. I
Discipleship in the New Age — Vol. II
Problems of Humanity
The Reappearance of the Christ
The Destiny of the Nations
Glamour: A World Problem
Telepathy and the Etheric Vehicle
The Unfinished Autobiography
Education in the New Age
The Externalisation of the Hierarchy
A Treatise on the Seven Rays:
Vol. I — Esoteric Psychology
Vol. II — Esoteric Psychology
Vol. III — Esoteric Astrology
Vol. IV — Esoteric Healing
Vol. V — The Rays and the Initiations

THE GREAT INVOCATION

From the point of Light within the Mind of God
    Let light stream forth into the minds of men.
        Let Light descend on Earth.

From the point of Love within the Heart of God
    Let love stream forth into the hearts of men.
        May Christ return to Earth.

From the centre where the Will of God is known
    Let purpose guide the little wills of men —
        The purpose which the Masters know and serve.

From the centre which we call the race of men
    Let the Plan of Love and Light work out
        And may it seal the door where evil dwells.

Let Light and Love and Power restore the Plan on Earth.

"The above Invocation or Prayer does not belong to any person or group but to all Humanity. The beauty and the strength of this Invocation lies in its simplicity, and in its expression of certain central truths which all men, innately and normally, accept — the truth of the existence of a basic Intelligence to Whom we vaguely give the name of God; the truth that behind all outer seeming, the motivating power of the universe is Love; the truth that a great Individuality came to earth, called by Christians, the Christ, and embodied that love so that we could understand; the truth that both love and intelligence are effects of what is called the Will of God; and finally the self-evident truth that only through *humanity* itself can the Divine Plan work out."

ALICE A. BAILEY

EXTRACT FROM A STATEMENT BY THE TIBETAN

Suffice it to say, that I am a Tibetan disciple of a certain degree, and this tells you but little, for all are disciples from the humblest aspirant up to, and beyond, the Christ Himself. I live in a physical body like other men, on the borders of Tibet, and at times (from the exoteric standpoint) preside over a large group of Tibetan lamas, when my other duties permit. It is this fact that has caused it to be reported that I am an abbot of this particular lamasery. Those associated with me in the work of the Hierarchy (and all true disciples are associated in this work) know me by still another name and office. A.A.B. knows who I am and recognises me by two of my names.

I am a brother of yours, who has travelled a little longer upon the Path than has the average student, and has therefore incurred greater responsibilities. I am one who has wrestled and fought his way into a greater measure of light than has the aspirant who will read this article, and I must therefore act as a transmitter of the light, no matter what the cost. I am not an old man, as age counts among teachers, yet I am not young or inexperienced. My work is to teach and spread the knowledge of the Ageless Wisdom wherever I can find a response, and I have been doing this for many years. I seek also to help the Master M. and the Master K.H. whenever opportunity offers, for I have been long connected with Them and with Their work. In all the above, I have told you much; yet at the same time I have told you nothing which would lead you to offer me that blind obedience and the foolish devotion which the emotional aspirant offers to the Guru and Master Whom he is as yet unable to contact. Nor will he make that desired contact until he has transmuted emotional devotion into unselfish service to humanity,—not to the Master.

The books that I have written are sent out with no claim for their acceptance. They may, or may not, be correct, true and useful. It is for you to ascertain their truth by right practice and by the exercise of the intuition. Neither I nor A.A.B. is the least interested in having them acclaimed as inspired writings, or in having anyone speak of them (with bated breath) as being the work of one of the Masters. If they present truth in such a way that it follows sequentially upon that already offered in the world teachings, if the information given raises the aspiration and the will-to-serve from the plane of the emotions to that of the mind (the plane whereon the Masters *can* be found) then they will have served their purpose. If the teaching conveyed calls forth a response from the illumined mind of the worker in the world, and brings a flashing forth of his intuition, then let that teaching be accepted. But not otherwise. If the statements meet with eventual corroboration, or are deemed true under the test of the Law of Correspondences, then that is well and good. But should this not be so, let not the student accept what is said.

August 1934

TABLE OF CONTENTS

CHAPTER I
THE DOCTRINE OF THE COMING ONE 5

CHAPTER II
CHRIST'S UNIQUE OCCASION 15

CHAPTER III
THE REAPPEARANCE OF THE CHRIST 36

CHAPTER IV
THE WORK OF THE CHRIST 61

CHAPTER V
THE TEACHINGS OF THE CHRIST 102

CHAPTER VI
THE NEW WORLD RELIGION 137

CHAPTER VII
PREPARATION FOR THE CHRIST 160

CONCLUSION 187

INDEX 193

KEYNOTE

Whenever there is a withering of the law and an uprising of lawlessness on all sides, *then* I manifest Myself.

For the salvation of the righteous and the destruction of such as do evil, for the firm establishing of the Law, I come to birth age after age.

THE BHAGAVAD GITA
Book IV, Sutra 7, 8.

CHAPTER ONE

THE DOCTRINE OF THE COMING ONE
Western Teaching
THE DOCTRINE OF AVATARS
Eastern Teaching

RIGHT down the ages, in many world cycles and in many countries (and today in all) great points of tension have occurred which have been characterised by a hopeful sense of expectancy. Some one is expected and His coming is anticipated. Always in the past, it has been the religious teachers of the period who have fostered and proclaimed this expectancy and the time has always been one of chaos and difficulty, of a climaxing point at the close of a civilisation or culture and when the resources of the old religions have seemed inadequate to meet men's difficulties or to solve their problems. The coming of the Avatar, the advent of a Coming One and, in terms of today, the reappearance of the Christ are the keynotes of the prevalent expectancy. When the times are ripe, the invocation of the masses is strident enough and the faith of those who know is keen enough, *then* always He has come and today will be no exception to this ancient rule or to this universal law. For decades, the reappearance of the Christ, the Avatar, has been anticipated by the faithful in both hemispheres—not only by the Christian faithful, but by those who look for Maitreya and for the Boddhisattva as well as those who expect the Imam Mahdi.

When men feel that they have exhausted all their own resources and have come to an end of all their own innate possibilities and that the problems and conditions confronting them are beyond their solving or handling, they are apt to look for a divine Intermediary and for the

Mediator Who will plead their cause with God and bring about a rescue. They look for a Saviour. This doctrine of Mediators, of Messiahs, of Christs and of Avatars can be found running like a golden thread through all the world faiths and Scriptures and, relating these world Scriptures to some central source of emanation, they are found in rich abundance everywhere. Even the human soul is regarded as an intermediary between man and God; Christ is believed by countless millions to act as the divine mediator between humanity and divinity.

The whole system of spiritual revelation is based (and has always been based) on this doctrine of interdependence, of a planned and arranged conscious linking and of the transmission of energy from one aspect of divine manifestation to another—from God in the "secret Place of the Most High" to the humblest human being, living and struggling and sorrowing on earth. Everywhere this transmission is to be found; "I am come that they may have life" says the Christ, and the Scriptures of the world are full of the intervention of some Being, originating from some source higher than the strictly human. Always the appropriate mechanism is found through which divinity can reach and communicate with humanity, and it is with this communication and these Instruments of divine energy that the doctrine of Avatars or of divine "Coming Ones" has to do.

An Avatar is one Who has a peculiar capacity (besides a self-initiated task and a pre-ordained destiny) to transmit energy or divine power. This is necessarily a deep mystery and was demonstrated in a peculiar manner and in relation to cosmic energy by the Christ Who—for the first time in planetary history, as far as we know—transmitted the divine energy of *love* directly to our planet and in a most definite sense to humanity. Always too these Avatars or divine Messengers are linked with the concept of some subjective spiritual Order or Hierarchy of spiritual Lives, Who are concerned with the developing welfare of humanity. All *really know* is that, down the ages, great and divine Representatives of God embody divine purpose, and affect the entire world in such a manner that Their names and Their influence are known and felt thousands of years after They no longer walk among men. Again and again, They have come and have left a changed world and some new world religion behind Them; we know also that prophecy and faith have ever held out to mankind the promise of Their coming again amongst us in an hour of need. These statements are statements of fact, historically proven. Beyond this we know relatively few details.

The word "Avatar" is a Sanskrit word, meaning literally "coming down from far away." *Ava* (as prefix to verbs and verbal nouns) expresses the idea of "off, away, down." *Avataram* (comparative) farther away. The root AV seems at all times to denote the *idea of protection from above*, and is used in compounds, in words referring to protections by kings or rulers; in regard to the gods, it means accepted favorably when a sacrifice is offered. With the result that the root word can be said to mean "Coming down with the approval of the higher source from which it came and with benefit to the place at which it arrives." (From *Monier-Williams' Sanskrit Dictionary.*)

All the world Avatars or Saviours, however, express two basic incentives: the need of God to contact humanity and to have relationship with men and the need of humanity for divine contact, help and understanding. Subject to those incentives, all true Avatars are therefore divine Intermediaries. They can act in this fashion because They have completely divorced Themselves from every limitation, from all sense of selfhood and separativeness and are no longer—by ordinary human standards—the dramatic centre of Their lives, as are most of us. When They have reached that stage of spiritual decentralization, They Themselves can then become *events* in the life of our planet; toward Them every eye can look and all men can be affected. Therefore, an Avatar or a Christ comes forth for two reasons: one, the inscrutable and unknown Cause prompts Him so to do, and the other is the demand or the invocation of humanity itself. An Avatar is consequently a spiritual event, coming to us to bring about great changes or major restorations, to inaugurate a new civilisation or to restore the "ancient landmarks" and lead man nearer to the divine. They have been defined as "extraordinary men Who from time to time appear to change the face of the world and inaugurate a new era in the destinies of humanity." They come in times of crisis; They frequently create crises in order to bring to an end the old and the undesirable and make way for new and more suitable forms for the evolving life of God Immanent in Nature. They come when evil is rampant. For this reason, if for no other, an Avatar may be looked for today. The necessary stage is set for the reappearance of the Christ.

Avatars are of all degrees and kinds; some of them are of great planetary importance because They express whole cycles of future development within Themselves and strike the note and give the teaching which will bring in a new age and a new civilisation; They embody great truths towards which the masses of men must work and which still constitute an objective to the greatest minds of the age, even though as yet unrealised. Certain Avatars also express in Themselves the sumtotal of human achieve-

THE DOCTRINE OF THE COMING ONE

ment and of racial perfection, and thus become the "ideal men" of the ages. Others, greater still, are permitted to be the custodians of some divine principle or some divine quality which needs fresh presentation and expression upon Earth; this They can be because They have achieved perfection and have attained to the highest possible initiations. They have the gift of *being* these embodied spiritual qualities, and because They have in fullness expressed such a specific principle or quality They can act as channels for its transmission from the centre of all spiritual Life. This is the basis for the doctrine of Avatars or Divine Messengers.

Such an one was the Christ; He was twice an Avatar because He not only struck the keynote of the new age (over two thousand years ago) but He also, in some mysterious and incomprehensible manner, embodied in Himself the divine Principle of Love; He was the first to reveal to men the true nature of God. The invocative cry of humanity (the second of the incentives producing a divine Emergence) is potent in effect because the souls of men, particularly in concerted action, have in them something which is akin to the divine nature of the Avatar. We are all Gods, all the children of the One Father, as the latest of the Avatars, the Christ, has told us. It is that divine centre in every human heart which, when awakened into activity, can call forth response from the high Place where the Coming One awaits His hour of appearance. It is only the united demand of humanity, its "massed intent," which can precipitate the descent (as it is called) of an Avatar.

To sum up, therefore: the doctrine of Avatars is paralleled by *the doctrine of the continuity of revelation.* Ever down the ages, and at every great human crisis, always in the hours of necessity, at the founding of a new race, or in the awakening of a prepared humanity to a new and wider vision, the Heart of God—impelled by the Law of Compassion—sends forth a Teacher, a world Saviour, an Illuminator, an Avatar, a transmitting Intermediary, a Christ. He gives the message which will heal, which will indicate the next step to be taken by the race of men, which will illumine a dark world problem and give to man an expression of some hitherto unrealised aspect of divinity. Upon this fact of the continuity of revelation and upon the sequence of this progressive manifestation of the divine Nature, is based the doctrine of Avatars, divine Messengers, divine Appearances and Saviours. To Them all, history unmistakenly testifies. It is upon the fact of this continuity, this sequence of Messengers and Avatars, and upon the dire and dreadful need of humanity at this time, that the worldwide expectancy of the reappearance of the Christ is based. It is the innate recognition of all these facts that has led to the steadily mounting invocative cry of humanity in every land for some form of divine relief or divine intervention; it is the recognition of these facts which also prompts the order which has gone forth from "the centre where the will of God is known" that the Avatar should come again; it is the knowledge of both these demands which has led the Christ to let His disciples in every land *know* that He will re-appear when they have done the needed preparatory work.

The Avatars most easily known and recognised are the Buddha in the East and the Christ in the West. Their messages are familiar to all, and the fruits of Their lives and words have conditioned the thinking and civilisations of both hemispheres. Because They are human-divine Avatars, They represent what humanity can easily understand; because They are of like nature to us, "flesh of

THE DOCTRINE OF THE COMING ONE 11

our flesh and spirit of our spirit," we know and trust Them and They mean more to us than other divine Emergences. They are known, trusted and loved by countless millions. The nucleus of spiritual energy which each of Them set up is beyond our measuring; *the establishing of a nucleus of persistent energy, spiritually positive, is the constant task of an Avatar;* He focusses or anchors a dynamic truth, a potent thoughtform or a vortex of magnetic energy in the world of human living. This focal point acts increasingly as a transmitter of spiritual energy; it enables humanity to express some divine idea and this in time produces a civilisation with its accompanying culture, religions, policies, governments and educational processes. Thus is history made. History is after all only the record of humanity's cyclic reaction to some inflowing divine energy, to some inspired leader, or to some Avatar.

An Avatar is at present usually a Representative of the second divine aspect, that of Love-Wisdom, the Love of God. He will manifest as the Saviour, the Builder, the Preserver; humanity is not yet sufficiently developed or adequately oriented to the life of the Spirit to bear easily the impact of an Avatar Who would express the dynamic will of God. For us as yet (and this is *our* limitation) an Avatar is one Who preserves, develops, builds, protects, shields and succours the spiritual impulses by which men live; that which brings Him into manifestation is man's need and man's demand for preservation and help. Humanity needs love, understanding and right human relations as an expression of attained divinity. It was this need which brought the Christ to us before as the Avatar of Love. The Christ, that great human-divine Messenger, because of His stupendous achievement—along the line of understanding—transmitted to humanity an aspect and a potency of the nature of God Himself, the *love* Principle of Deity. Light, aspiration, and the recognition of God Transcendent had been the flickering expression of the human attitude to God, prior to the advent of the Buddha, the Avatar of Illumination. Then the Buddha came and demonstrated in His Own life the fact of God Immanent as well as God Transcendent, of God in the universe and of God within humanity. The Selfhood of Deity and the Self in the heart of individual man became a factor in human consciousness. It was a relatively new truth to man.

However, until Christ came and lived a life of love and service and gave men the new command to love one another, there had been very little emphasis upon God as Love in any of the world Scriptures. After He had come as the Avatar of Love, then God became known as love supernal, love as the goal and objective of creation, love as the basic principle of relationship and love as working throughout all manifestation towards a Plan motivated by love. This divine quality, Christ revealed and emphasised and thus altered all human living, goals and values.

The reason He has not come again is that the needed work has not been done by His followers in all countries. His coming is largely dependent, as we shall later see, upon the establishing of right human relations. This the church has hindered down the centuries, and has not helped because of its fanatical zeal to make "Christians" of all peoples and not followers of the Christ. It has emphasised theological doctrine, and not love and loving understanding as Christ exemplified it. The Church has preached the fiery Saul of Tarsus and not the gentle Carpenter of Galilee. And so, He has waited. But His hour has now come, because of the people's need in every

THE DOCTRINE OF THE COMING ONE 13

land and because of the invocative cry of the masses everywhere and the advice of His disciples of all faiths and of all world religions.

It is not for us yet to know the date or the hour of the reappearance of the Christ. His coming is dependent upon the appeal (the often voiceless appeal) of all who stand with massed intent; it is dependent also upon the better establishment of right human relations and upon certain work being done at this time by senior Members of the Kingdom of God, the Church Invisible, the spiritual Hierarchy of our planet; it is dependent also upon the steadfastness of the Christ's disciples in the world at this time and His initiate-workers—all working in the many groups, religious, political and economic. To the above must be added what Christians like to call "the inscrutable Will of God," that unrecognised purpose of the Lord of the World, the Ancient of Days (as He is called in *The Old Testament*) Who "knows His own Mind, radiates the highest quality of love and focusses His Will in His Own high Place within the centre where the Will of God is known."

When the Christ, the Avatar of Love, makes His reappearance then will the

"Sons of men who are now the Sons of God withdraw Their faces from the shining light and radiate that light upon the *sons of men who know not yet they are the Sons of God.* Then shall the Coming One appear, His footsteps hastened through the valley of the shadow by the One of awful power Who stands upon the mountain top, breathing out love eternal, light supernal and peaceful, silent Will.

"Then will the sons of men respond. Then will a newer light shine forth into the dismal, weary vale of earth. Then will new life course through the veins of men, and then will their vision compass all the ways of what may be.

"So peace will come again on earth, but a peace unlike aught known before. Then will the will-to-good flower forth as understanding, and understanding blossom as goodwill in men."

CHAPTER TWO

CHRIST'S UNIQUE OCCASION
The World Today

IN any acceptance of the teaching that Christ will come, one of the difficulties today is the feeling that the teaching has been given for many centuries and nothing has ever happened. That is a statement of fact, and here lies a great deal of our trouble. The expectancy of His coming is nothing new; in it lies nothing unique or different; those who still hold to the idea are regarded tolerantly, or with amusement or pity, as the case may be. A study of times and seasons, of significances, of divine intention or of the will of God, plus a consideration of the world situation, may lead us, however, to believe that *the present time is unique* in more ways than one, and that the Christ is confronted with an unique occasion. This unique opportunity with which He is presented is brought about by certain world conditions which themselves are unique; there are factors present in the world today, and happenings have taken place within the past century which have never before occurred; it might profit us if we considered these matters and so gained a better perspective. The world to which He will come is a new world, if not yet a better world; new ideas are occupying people's minds and new problems await solution. Let us look at this uniqueness and gain some knowledge of the situation into which the Christ will be precipitated. Let us be realistic in our approach to this theme and avoid mystical and vague thinking. If it is true that He plans to reappear, if it is a fact that He will bring His disciples, the Masters of the Wisdom, with Him, and if this coming is imminent, what are some of the factors which He and they must take into consideration?

First of all, He will come to a world which is essentially one world. His reappearance and His consequent work cannot be confined to one small locality or domain unheard of by the great majority, as was the case when He was here before. The radio, the press and the dissemination of news will make His coming different to that of any previous Messenger; the swift modes of transportation will make Him available to countless millions, and by boat, rail and plane they can reach Him: through television, His face can be made familiar to all, and verily "every eye shall see Him." Even if there is no general recognition of His spiritual status and His message, there must necessarily be an universal interest, for today even the many false Christs and Messengers are finding this universal curiosity and cannot be hidden. This creates an unique condition in which to work, and one which no salvaging, energising Son of God has ever before had to face.

The sensitivity of the people of the world to what is new or needed is also uniquely different; man has progressed far in his reaction to both good and evil and possesses a far more sensitive response apparatus than did humanity in those earlier times. If there was a quick response to the Messenger when He came before, it will be more general and quicker now, both in rejection and in acceptance. Men are more enquiring, better educated, more intuitive and more expectant of the unusual and the unique than at any other time in history. Their intellectual perception is keener, their sense of values more acute, their ability to discriminate and choose is fast developing.

CHRIST'S UNIQUE OCCASION

and they penetrate more quickly into significances. These facts will condition the reappearance of the Christ and tend to a more rapid spreading of the news of His coming and the contents of His message.

Today, when He comes, He will find a world uniquely free from the grip and hold of ecclesiasticism; when He came before, Palestine was held in the vicious grasp of the Jewish religious leaders, and the Pharisees and the Sadducees were to the people of that land what the potentates of the church are to the people in the world today. But—there has been a useful and wholesome swing away from Churchianity and from orthodox religion during the past century, and this will present a unique opportunity for the restoration of true religion and the presentation of a simple return to the ways of spiritual living. The priests, the Levites, the Pharisees and the Sadducees were not the ones who recognised Him when He came before. They feared Him. And it is highly improbable that the reactionary churchmen will be the ones to recognise Him today. He may reappear in a totally unexpected guise; who is to say whether He will come as a politician, an economist, a leader of the people (arising from the midst of them), a scientist or an artist?

It is a fallacy to believe, as some do, that the main trend of Christ's work will be through the medium of the churches or the world religions. He necessarily will work through them when conditions permit and there is a living nucleus of true spirituality within them, or when their invocative appeal is potent enough to reach Him. He will use all possible channels whereby the consciousness of man may be enlarged and right orientation be brought about. It is, however, truer to say that it is as World Teacher that He will consistently work, and that the churches are but one of the teaching avenues He will employ. All that enlightens the minds of men, all propaganda that tends to bring about right human relations, all modes of acquiring real knowledge, all methods of transmuting knowledge into wisdom and understanding, all that expands the consciousness of humanity and of all subhuman states of awareness and sensitivity, all that dispels glamour and illusion and that disrupts crystallisation and disturbs static conditions will come under the realistic activities of the Hierarchy which He supervises. He will be limited by the quality and the calibre of the invocative appeal of humanity and that, in its turn, is conditioned by the attained point in evolution.

In the Middle Ages of history and earlier, it was the churches and the schools of philosophy which provided the major avenues for His subjective activity, but it will not be so when He is objectively and actually here. This is a point which the churches and organised religions would do well to remember. There is now a shift of His emphasis and attention into two new fields of endeavour: first, into the field of world-wide education, and secondly, into the sphere of implementing intelligently those activities which come under the department of government in its three aspects of statesmanship, of politics and of legislation. The common people are today awakening to the importance and responsibility of government; it is, therefore, realised by the Hierarchy that before the cycle of true democracy (as it essentially exists and will eventually demonstrate) can come into being, the education of the masses in cooperative statesmanship, in economic stabilisation through right sharing, and in clean, political interplay is imperatively necessary. The long divorce between religion and politics *must* be ended and this can now come about because of the high level of the human *mass* intelligence and the fact that science has made all men so close

CHRIST'S UNIQUE OCCASION

that what happens in some remote area of the earth's surface is a matter of general interest within a few minutes. This makes it uniquely possible for Him to work in the future.

The development of spiritual recognition is the great need today in preparation for His reappearance; no one knows in what nation He will come; He may appear as an Englishman, a Russian, a Negro, a Latin, a Turk, a Hindu, or any other nationality. Who can say which? He may be a Christian or a Hindu by faith, a Buddhist or of no particular faith at all; He will not come as the restorer of any of the ancient religions, including Christianity, but He will come to restore man's faith in the Father's love, in the fact of the livingness of the Christ and in the close, subjective and unbreakable relationship of all men everywhere. The facilities of the entire world of contact and relation will be at His disposal; that will be part of the uniqueness of His opportunity and—for this He too must prepare.

Another unique factor which will distinguish His coming will be not only the general expectancy but also the fact that much is today known and taught about the Kingdom of God, or the Spiritual Hierarchy of the planet. Everywhere, in all countries, there are thousands who are interested in the fact of that Hierarchy, who believe in the Masters of the Wisdom, the disciples of the Christ, and who will not be surprised when this group of Sons of God, surrounding their great Leader, the Christ, makes its appearance on Earth. The churches in all countries have familiarised the public with the phrase "the Kingdom of God"; the esotericists and occultists everywhere have publicised the fact of the Hierarchy during the past century; the spiritualists have laid the emphasis upon the aliveness of those who have passed over into the hidden world of being, and their Guides have also borne testimony to the existence of an inner, spiritual world. All this creates a unique preparedness which presents the Christ with unique opportunities and unique problems. All these spiritual forces and many others, both within and without the world religions and the philosophical and humanitarian groups, are working at this time under direction, are closely related and their activities most intimately synchronised. They are all working *together* (even if this is not physically apparent) because in the human family there are those at every stage of responsiveness. The forces of regeneration, of reconstruction, of restoration and of resurrection are making their presence felt in all the many groups which are seeking to aid and lift humanity, to rebuild the world, to restore stability and the sense of security and thus (consciously or unconsciously) prepare the way for the coming of the Christ.

There is also a unique revival of the ancient teaching of the Buddha and it is penetrating into the Western countries and finding devoted adherents in every land. The Buddha is the symbol of enlightenment and there is everywhere today a unique emphasis upon *light*. Countless millions down the ages have recognised the Buddha as the Light Bearer from on high. His *Four Noble Truths* exposed the causes of human trouble and pointed to the cure. He taught: Cease to identify yourselves with material things or with your desires; gain a proper sense of value; cease regarding possessions and earthly existence as of major importance; follow the Noble Eightfold Path which is the Path of right relations—right relations to God, and right relations to your fellow men—and thus be happy. The steps on this Path are:

CHRIST'S UNIQUE OCCASION

Right Values.	Right Aspiration.
Right Speech.	Right Conduct.
Right Modes of Living.	Right Effort.
Right Thinking.	Right Rapture or Happiness.

This message is uniquely needed today in a world in which most of these right steps to happiness have been consistently ignored. It is on the foundation of this teaching that Christ will raise the superstructure of the brotherhood of man, for right human relations are an expression of the love of God; they will constitute man's major and next demonstration of divinity. Today, in the midst of this devastated, chaotic and unhappy world, mankind has a fresh opportunity to reject selfish materialistic living and to begin to tread the Lighted Way. The moment that humanity shows its willingness to do this, *then* the Christ will come, and there is every evidence at this time that men are learning this lesson and making their first faltering steps along that Lighted Way of right relationships.

The present time is unique in that it is (as never before) a cycle or period of conferences—communal, national and international—and of men getting together. Clubs, forums, committees, conferences, and leagues are forming everywhere for the discussion and study of human welfare and liberation; this phenomenon is one of the strongest indications that the Christ is on His way. He is the embodiment of freedom, and the Messenger of Liberation. He stimulates the group spirit and the group consciousness, and His spiritual energy is the attractive force, binding men together for the common good. His reappearance will knit and bind together all men and women of goodwill throughout the world, irrespective of religion or nationality. His coming will evoke among men a widespread and mutual recognition of the good in all. This is part of the uniqueness of His coming and for it we are already preparing. A study of the daily press will prove this. It is the invocative appeal of the many groups working on behalf of humanity (consciously or unconsciously made) which will bring Him forth. Those who carry out this great act of invocation are the spiritually minded people, the enlightened statesmen, the religious leaders and the men and women whose hearts are full of goodwill. They will evoke Him *if* they can stand with massed intent, with hope and with expectancy. This preparatory work must be focussed through and implemented by the world intelligentsia and leading lovers of humanity, by groups dedicated to human betterment and by representative unselfish people. The success of the effort now being planned by Christ and the spiritual Hierarchy is dependent upon the ability of mankind to use what light it already has in order to establish right relations in their families, their community, in their nation and in the world.

There is, therefore, this unique difference between the expected coming of the Christ and the time when He came before: the world is full of groups working for human welfare. This effort, in the light of past aeons of human history, is a relatively new thing and for it the Christ must prepare and with this trend He will have to work. The "cycle of conferences" which is now swinging into full tide is part of the unique condition with which the Christ is faced.

Before, however, Christ could come with His disciples, our present civilisation had to die. During the coming century, we shall begin to learn the meaning of the word "resurrection," and the new age will begin to reveal its deep purpose and intention. The first step will be the emergence of humanity from the death of its civilisation,

CHRIST'S UNIQUE OCCASION 23

of its old ideas and modes of living, the relinquishing of its materialistic goals and its damning selfishness, and its moving forward into the clear light of the resurrection. These are not symbolical or mystical words but part of the general setting which will surround the period of Christ's reappearance; it is a cycle as real as the cycle of conferences now so busily organising. Christ taught us when He came before the true meaning of Renunciation or of the Crucifixion; this time His message will be concerned with *the resurrection life.* The present cycle of conferences is preparing men everywhere for relationships, even though today they may seem widely divergent in nature; the important factor is the general human interest and thought about establishing the need, the objectives involved, the means to be employed. The resurrection period which the Christ will inaugurate and which will constitute His unique work—within which all His other activities will have their place—will be the outcome of the fermentation and the germination going on in the world of men at this time, of which the many conferences are the outer evidence.

It was these various unique conditions which the Christ faced during the years of war when the need of humanity forced Him to decide to hasten His coming. The unhappy state of the world as the result of centuries of selfishness and of the world war, the unique sensitivity which men everywhere were showing (as a result of the evolutionary process) the unique spread of knowledge about the spiritual Hierarchy and the unique development of group consciousness, showing itself on every hand in the multiplicity of conferences, confronted Christ with His unique occasion and presented Him with a decision which He could not avoid.

Reverently we might say that in this "occasion" of the Christ's, two facts were involved and that both of them are difficult for man to understand. The fact of the synchronisation of His will with that of the Father, and the fact that this synchronisation led to a basic decision, must be recognised by us. It is not easy for the average Christian to realise that the Christ passes on steadily to increasingly potent experiences, and that in His divine experience there is nothing static or permanent —except His unalterable love for humanity.

A close study of the Gospel story, unimpeded by orthodox interpretations, reveals certain things. The usual interpretations, if men would but recognise them in their true meaning, are simply some man's understanding of a series of Aramaic, Greek or Latin words. The fact that the majority of accepted commentators lived many hundreds of years ago seems to have given such words a totally unwarranted value. The words of a commentator or of an interpreter today are apparently of no value in comparison with those of ancient date; yet the modern commentator is probably more intelligent and better educated than the ancient one and has, also, the benefit of the many recognised translations and a precise science. We are suffering theologically from the ignorance of the past; it is a peculiar thing that an ancient commentator is supposed to carry greater weight than the modern, more educated and intelligent man. If *The New Testament* is true in its presentation of the Christ, if it is true in its repetition of His words, that we can do "greater things" than He did, and if it is true in that He told us to "be perfect even as our Father in Heaven is perfect," what is there wrong in our recognising the capacity of a human being to keep pace with the mind of Christ and to know what He intends us to know? Christ said that "if any

CHRIST'S UNIQUE OCCASION

man will do the will of God, he shall know"; that was how the Christ Himself learnt and that is the mode He assures us will be successful for each of us.

It was the dawning of this significance of the will of God upon the consciousness of the Christ which led Him to certain great decisions, and which forced Him to cry out: "Father, not my will but Thine be done." These words definitely indicate conflict and do not indicate the synchronisation of the two wills; they indicate the determination on the part of the Christ that there should be no opposition between His will and that of God. Suddenly, He received a vision of the emerging, divine intention for humanity and—through humanity—for the planet as a whole. At the particular stage of spiritual development which Christ had then attained and which had made Him the Head of the spiritual Hierarchy, the One who engineered the emergence of the Kingdom of God and established Him as the Master of all the Masters and the Teacher of angels and of men, His consciousness was absolutely at one with the divine Plan; its application on Earth and its goal of establishing the Kingdom of God and the appearance of the fifth kingdom in nature was simply for Him the fulfilling of the law and to that fulfillment His entire life was and had been geared.

The Plan, its goal, its techniques and its laws, its energy (that of love) and the close and growing relation between the spiritual Hierarchy and humanity were known to him, and fully understood. At the highest point of this consummated knowledge and at the moment of His complete surrender to the necessary sacrifice of His life to the fulfilling of this Plan, suddenly a great expansion of consciousness took place. The significance, the intention, the purpose of it all, and the comprehensive divine Idea (as it existed in the mind of the Father) dawned upon His soul—not on His mind, for the revelation was far greater than that. He saw still further into the meaning of divinity than had ever before seemed possible; the world of meaning and the world of phenomena faded out and—esoterically speaking—He lost His all. For the time being, neither the energy of the creative mind nor the energy of love were left to Him. He was bereft of all that had made life bearable and full of meaning. A new type of energy became available— the energy of life itself, *imbued with purpose and actuated by intention*. But it was new and unknown and hitherto unrealised. For the first time, the relation of the *will* which had hitherto expressed itself in His life through love and the creative work of inaugurating the new dispensation became clear to Him. At this point, He passed through the Gethsemane of renunciation. The greater, the larger and the more inclusive was revealed to Him and all that hitherto seemed so vital and important was lost to sight in the greater vision. It is this living realisation of Being and of identification with the divine intention of God Himself, the Father, the Lord of the World upon levels of awareness of which we know nothing (as yet) which constituted the unfolding awareness of the Christ upon the Way of the Higher Evolution. This Way He treads today and He began to tread it in Palestine two thousand years ago. He *knew,* in a sense hitherto unknown to Him, what God intended and what human destiny meant, and the part that He had to play in the working out of that destiny. We have paid little attention down the centuries of human thinking to Christ's reaction to His own destiny, as it affected the human. We have paid small attention to the aspect of His reaction to knowledge, as it unfolded itself to

CHRIST'S UNIQUE OCCASION 27

Him. We have been selfish and grasping in our reaction to His work and sacrifice.

The word to *"know"* (in relation to the initiate-consciousness of the Christ and of still lesser initiates) concerns the certainty of the knowledge the initiate has gained through experiment, experience and expression. The first faint tremor of reaction to monadic "destiny" and to the widespread universal influence a Son of God can exert makes itself felt in the consciousness of the Christ—as it will in the consciousness of all those who obey His injunction and arrive at the perfection which He pointed out as possible. The highest divine quality or aspect now makes itself felt in the life of the progressing Son of God; He knows the meaning of intelligence; He realises the significance of love and its attractive quality. Now—because of these two recognitions—He becomes aware of the potency of will and of the reality of the divine intention which that will must (at any cost) implement. This was the major crisis of the Christ.

There are in the Gospel story (as testimony to this divinely progressing unfoldment) four recorded moments wherein this universal or monadic realisation showed itself. Let us look at each one of them for a moment:—

1. There is, first of all, His statement to His parents in the Temple, "Wist ye not that I must be about my Father's business?" We should note here that He was twelve years old at the time and, therefore, the work with which He had been occupied (as a soul) was finished; twelve is the number of completed work, as witness the twelve labours of Hercules, another Son of God. The symbolism of His twelve years is now replaced by that of the twelve apostles, the symbol of service and sacrifice. He was also in the Temple of Solomon, which is the symbol

of the perfect life of the soul, just as the Tabernacle in the wilderness is the symbol of the imperfect ephemeral life of the transient personality; Christ was, therefore, speaking on soul levels and not only as the spiritual man on Earth. He was also serving, when He spoke these words, as a working Member of the Spiritual Hierarchy, for He was found by His parents teaching the priests, the Pharisees and the Sadducees. These points all indicate His recognition of His work as a World Teacher, becoming conscious, for the first time in His physical brain, of divine intention or of the divine will.

2. Next comes His statement to His disciples: "I must go up to Jerusalem," after which we read that He "steadfastly set His face to go" to that city. This was the intimation to them that He now had a new objective. The only place of complete "peace" (which is the meaning of the name "Jerusalem") is the "centre where the will of God is known." The spiritual Hierarchy of our planet (the invisible Church of Christ) is not a centre of peace but a very vortex of loving activity, the meeting place of energies coming from the centre of the divine will, and from humanity, the centre of divine intelligence. Christ had oriented Himself to that divine centre which has, in the ancient Scriptures, been called the "place of serene determination and of poised, quiescent will." This statement marked a point of crisis and of determination in the life of Christ, and proved His progress towards divine fulfillment.

3. Then in the Garden of Gethsemane He said, "Father, not My will but Thine be done," thus indicating His realisation of divine destiny. The meaning of these words is not (as is so often stated by Christian

CHRIST'S UNIQUE OCCASION

theologians) a statement of acceptance of pain and of an unpleasant future and of death. It was an exclamation, evoked surely by His realisation of the universal implications of His mission and the intense focussing of His life in a universal sense. The Gethsemane experience was an experience uniquely possible only to those Sons of God Who have reached His rare point in evolution; it had no real relation to the Crucifixion episode, as the orthodox commentators emphasise.

4. The final words of the Christ to His apostles were, "Lo, I am with you all the days, even unto the end of the age" or cycle. (Matt. 28.20) The important word is "end." The word used is the Greek "sun-teleia," which means the end of the time period, with another immediately following after (what would be called the end of a cycle). In Greek the final *end* is another word "telos." In Matt. 24.6, "but the end is not yet," the other word *telos* is used for it means "the end of the first period has not yet been reached." Here He was speaking as the Head of the spiritual Hierarchy and expressing His divine will (at-one now with the will of God) to inform and pervade continuously the world of men with His overshadowing consciousness. It was a tremendous affirmation, sent forth upon the energy of His developed will, His all-inclusive love and His intelligent mind. This affirmation has made all things possible.

It was also to the magnetic power of the will that Christ referred when He said, "I, if I be lifted up, will draw all men unto Me." This had no reference to the crucifixion but to the magnetic will of the Christ to draw all men, through the life of the indwelling Christ in every heart, out of the world of material values into the world of spiritual recognitions. It did not relate to death but to life; it had no reference to the Cross but to the resurrection. In the past, the keynote of the Christian religion has been death, symbolised for us in the death of Christ and much distorted by ·St. Paul in his effort to blend the new religion which Christ brought with the old blood religion of the Jews. In the cycle which Christ will inaugurate after His reappearance, the goal of all the religious teaching in the world will be the resurrection of the spirit in mankind; the emphasis will be upon the livingness of the Christ nature in ·every human being, and upon *the use of the will in bringing about this living transfiguration* of the lower nature. The proof of it will be the risen Christ. This "Way of Resurrection" is the radiant Way, the lighted Way which leads from one great expression of divinity in man to another; it is the way which expresses the light of the intelligence, the radiant substance of true love, and the inflexible will which permits of no defeat or withdrawal. These are the characteristics which will be declarative of the Kingdom of God.

Today, humanity stands at a peculiar and unique middle point, between an unhappy past and a future which is full of promise if the reappearance of the Christ is recognised and preparation for His coming is undertaken. The present is full of promise and also full of difficulty; in the hands of human beings today and in the immediate present, lies the destiny of the world and—if it may be reverently said—the immediate activity of the Christ. The agony of the war, and the distress of the entire human family led Christ, in the year 1945, to come to a great decision—a decision which found expression in two most important statements. He announced to the assembled spiritual Hierarchy and to all His servants and disciples on Earth that He had decided to emerge again into physical contact with humanity, *if* they would bring

CHRIST'S UNIQUE OCCASION

about the initial stages of establishing right human relations; secondly, He gave to the world (for the use of the "man in the street") one of the oldest prayers ever known, but one which hitherto had not been permitted to be used except by the most exalted, spiritual Beings. He used it Himself for the first time, we are told, at the time of the Full Moon of June, 1945, which is recognised as the Full Moon of the Christ, just as the Full Moon of May is that of the Buddha. It was not easy to translate these ancient phrases (so ancient that they are without date or background of any kind) into modern words, but it has been done, and the great Invocation, which may eventually become the world prayer, was pronounced by Him and taken down by His disciples. It has been translated as follows:

From the point of Light within the Mind of God
   Let light stream forth into the minds of men.
   Let Light descend on Earth.

From the point of Love within the Heart of God
   Let love stream forth into the hearts of men.
   May Christ return to Earth.

From the centre where the Will of God is known
   Let purpose guide the little wills of men—
   The purpose which the Masters know and serve.

From the centre which we call the race of men
   Let the Plan of Love and Light work out
   And may it seal the door where evil dwells.

Let Light and Love and Power restore the Plan on Earth.

Its extraordinary potency can be seen in the fact that hundreds of thousands of people are already using it day by day and many times a day; it is (1947) translated into eighteen different languages and used by people in all those languages; in the jungles of Africa, groups of natives are using it and it can be seen on the desks of great executives in our major cities; it goes forth over the radio in Europe and in America and there is no country or island in the world where its use is unknown. All this has taken place in the space of eighteen months.

This new Invocation, if given widespread distribution, can be to the new world religion what the Lord's Prayer has been to Christianity and the 23rd Psalm has been to the spiritually minded Jew. There are three approaches to this great Prayer or Invocation:

1. That of the general public.
2. That of the esotericists, or of the aspirants and the disciples of the world.
3. That of the Members of the Hierarchy.

First, *the general public* will regard it as a prayer to God Transcendent. They will not recognise Him yet as immanent in His creation; they will send it forth on the wings of hope—hope for light and love and peace, for which they ceaselessly long. They will also regard it as a prayer for the enlightenment of all rulers and leaders in all groups who are handling world matters; as a prayer for the inflow of love and understanding among men, so that they may live in peace with one another; as a demand for the working out of the will of God—a will of which they can know nothing and which ever seems to them so inscrutable and so all-inclusive that their normal reaction is patience and a willingness to refrain from questioning; as a prayer for the strengthening of human responsibility in order that the recognised evils of today—which so distress and

CHRIST'S UNIQUE OCCASION

trouble mankind—may be done away with and some vague source of evil may be harnessed. They will regard it finally as a prayer that some equally vague primeval condition of blissful happiness may be restored and all unhappiness and pain disappear from the earth. This is, for them, entirely good and helpful and all that is immediately possible.

Secondly, *esotericists, aspirants and spiritually minded people* will have a deeper and more understanding approach. To them it will convey the recognition of the world of causes and of Those Who stand subjectively behind world affairs, the spiritual Directors of our life. They stand ready to strengthen those with true vision, ready to indicate not only the reason for events in the various departments of human living, but also to make those revelations which will enable humanity to move forward out of darkness into light. With this fundamental attitude, the necessity for a widespread expression of these underlying facts will be apparent and an era of spiritual propaganda, engineered by disciples and carried forward by esotericists, will mature. This era began in 1875 when the *fact* of the existence of the Masters of the Wisdom was proclaimed. It has been carried forward in spite of misrepresentation, attack upon the concept, and scorn. Recognition of the substantial nature of the available evidence and the appearance of an intuitive response by occult students and many of the intelligentsia throughout the world has been helpful.

A new type of mystic is coming to be recognised; he differs from the mystics of the past by his practical interest in current world affairs and not in religious and church matters only; he is distinguished by his lack of interest in his own personal development, by his ability to see God immanent in all faiths and not just in his own particular brand of religious belief, and also by his capacity to live his life in the light of the divine Presence. All mystics have been able to do this to a greater or less degree, but the modern mystic differs from those in the past in that *he is able clearly to indicate to others the techniques of the Path;* he combines both head and heart, intelligence and feeling, plus an intuitive perception, hitherto lacking. The clear light of the Spiritual Hierarchy now illumines the way of the modern mystic, and not simply the light of his own soul; this will be increasingly the case.

Thirdly, both of these groups—the general public and the world aspirants in their varying degrees—have, among them those who stand out from the general average as possessing a deeper insight and understanding; they occupy a no-man's-land, intermediate on the one hand between the masses and the esotericists and, on the other, between the esotericists and the Members of the Hierarchy. Forget not, They also use this great Invocation and that *not a day goes by that the Christ Himself does not sound it forth.*

On the surface, the beauty and the strength of this Invocation lie in its simplicity and in its expression of certain central truths which all men, innately and normally, accept—the truth of the existence of a basic Intelligence to Whom we vaguely give the name of *God;* the truth that, behind all outer seeming, the motivating power of the universe is *love;* the truth that a great Individuality came to earth, called by Christians the *Christ,* and embodied that love so that we could understand; the truth that both love and intelligence are effects of what is called the *will* of God, and finally the self-evident truth that only through *humanity* itself can the divine Plan work out.

CHRIST'S UNIQUE OCCASION

This Plan calls mankind to the expression of Love and challenges men to "let their light shine." Then comes the final solemn demand that this Plan of Love and Light, working through mankind, may "seal the door where evil dwells." The final line then contains *the idea of restoration,* indicating the keynote for the future and that the day will come when God's original idea and His initial intention will no longer be frustrated by human free will and evil—pure materialism and selfishness; the divine purpose will then, through the changed hearts and goals of humanity, be achieved.

This is the obvious and simple meaning and it ties in with the spiritual aspiration of all men everywhere.

The use of this Invocation or Prayer and the rising expectancy of the coming of the Christ hold out the greatest hope for mankind today. If this is not so, then prayer is no use and only an hallucination, and the Scriptures of the world, with their proved forecasting, are useless and deceiving. The testimony of the ages proves that *none of this is so*. Prayer always is answered and always has been; great Sons of God have ever come on humanity's demand and always will, and He for Whom all men wait today *is* on His way.

CHAPTER THREE

THE REAPPEARANCE OF THE CHRIST
World Expectancy

GOD Transcendent, greater, vaster and more inclusive than His created world, is universally recognised and has been generally emphasised; all faiths can say with Shri Krishna (speaking as God, the Creator) that "having pervaded the whole universe with a fragment of Myself, I remain." This God Transcendent has dominated the religious thinking of millions of simple and spiritually minded people down the centuries which have elapsed since humanity began to press forward towards divinity.

Slowly, there is dawning upon the awakening consciousness of humanity, the great paralleling truth of God Immanent—divinely "pervading" all forms, conditioning from within all kingdoms in nature, expressing innate divinity through human beings and—two thousand years ago—portraying the nature of that divine Immanence in the Person of the Christ. Today, as an outcome of this unfolding divine Presence, there is entering into the minds of men everywhere a new concept: that of "Christ in us, the hope of glory." (Col: 1.27.) There is a growing and developing belief that Christ *is* in us, as He was in the Master Jesus, and this belief will alter world affairs and mankind's entire attitude to life.

The wonder of that life, lived two thousand years ago, is still with us and has lost none of its freshness; it is an eternal inspiration, hope, encouragement and example. The love He demonstrated still holds the thinking world in thrall, even though relatively few have really attempted to demonstrate the same quality of love as He did—a love that leads unerringly to world service, to complete self-forgetfulness and to radiant, magnetic living. The words He spoke were few and simple and all men can understand them, but their significance has been largely lost in the intricate legalities and discussions of St. Paul, and in the lengthy disputation of theological commentators since Christ lived and left us—or apparently left us.

Yet—today Christ is nearer to humanity than at any other time in human history; He is closer than the most aspiring and hopeful disciple knows, and can draw closer still if what is here written is understood and brought to the attention of men everywhere. For Christ belongs to humanity, to the world of men, and not alone to the churches and religious faiths throughout the world.

Around Him—in that High Place on Earth where He has His abiding place—are gathered today all His great Disciples, the Masters of the Wisdom, and all Those liberated Sons of God Who, down the ages, have passed from darkness to Light, from the unreal to the Real, and from death to Immortality. They stand ready to carry out His bidding and to obey Him, the Master of all the Masters and the Teacher alike of Angels and of men. The Exponents and the Representatives of all the world faiths are there waiting, under His guidance, to reveal to all those who today struggle in the maelstrom of world affairs, and who seek to solve the world crisis, that *they are not alone*. God Transcendent is working through the Christ and the Spiritual Hierarchy to bring relief; God Immanent in all men is standing on the verge of certain stupendous Recognitions.

The great Apostolic Succession of the Knowers of God is poised today for renewed activity—a succession of Those Who have lived on Earth, accepted the fact of God Transcendent, discovered the reality of God Immanent, portrayed in Their own lives the divine characteristics of the Christ life and (because They lived on Earth as He did and does) have "entered for us within the veil, leaving us an example that we too should follow His steps" and Theirs. We too belong eventually in that great succession.

The Buddha Himself is standing behind the Christ in humble recognition of the divine task which He is on the verge of consummating, and because of the imminence of that spiritual accomplishment. Not only are all those who are functioning consciously in the Kingdom of God aware of His Plans, but those great spiritual Beings Who live and dwell in the "Father's House," in the "centre where the will of God is known," are also mobilised and organised to assist His work. The spiritual line of succession from the throne of the Ancient of Days down to the humblest disciple (gathered with others at the feet of the Christ) is today focussed on the task of helping humanity.

The great moment for which He has so patiently waited has almost arrived; the "end of the age" to which He referred when speaking to His small group of disciples: "Lo! I am with you all the days even unto the end of the age" has come. Today He stands and waits, knowing that the hour has come when He will "see of the travail of His soul and be satisfied." (Is:LIII:11.)

Right through the spiritual succession of the Sons of God, there is naught to be seen and felt but expectancy and preparation. *"The Hierarchy waits."* It has done all that is possible from the angle of the present opportunity. The Christ stands in patient silence, attentive to the effort that will make His work materialise on Earth and enable Him to consummate the effort He made 2000 years ago in Palestine. The Buddha hovers over the planet, ready to play His part if the opportunity is offered to Him by mankind. Everything now depends upon the right action of the men of goodwill.

From the Father's House (the "centre where the will of God is known" or Shamballa of the esotericist) the fiat has gone forth: The hour has come. From the Kingdom of God where reigns the Christ, the answer has been flung back: "Father, Thy will be done." Down in our struggling, bewildered, unhappy world of men, the cry is ceaselessly rising: "May Christ return to Earth." For the three great spiritual centres: the Father's House, the Kingdom of God, and awakening Humanity, there is but one purpose, one idea and one united expectancy.

It is essential that today there should be a measure of fuller knowledge concerning the "centre where the will of God is known." The public should possess some understanding of this highest spiritual centre to which—if we believe the Gospel story—Christ Himself was always attentive. Frequently we read in *The New Testament* that "the Father spoke to Him" or that "He heard a Voice," unheard by others, or that the words were heard, "this is my beloved Son." Several times, we read, the seal of affirmation (as it is spiritually called) was given to Him. Only the Father, the planetary Logos, the "One in Whom we live and move and have our being" (Acts XVII.28), the Lord of the World, the Ancient of Days (Dan. VII.9) can speak this final affirmative word. There are, as well we know, five crises or initiations which concern the Master Jesus—the Birth at Bethlehem, the Baptism, the Transfiguration, the Crucifixion and the Resurrection—but lying behind this obvious and practical teaching, lies an undercurrent or thought of something much higher and of greater importance—the affirmative Voice of the Father, recognising that which the Christ has done.

When Christ completes the work during the next two thousand years which He inaugurated two thousand years ago, that affirmative Voice will surely again be heard and divine recognition of His coming will be accorded. Then the Christ will take that stupendous initiation of which we know nothing except that two divine aspects will blend and fuse in Him (love-wisdom in full manifestation, motivated by divine will or power). Then the Buddha and the Christ will together pass before the Father, the Lord of the World, will together see the glory of the Lord and eventually pass to higher service of a nature and a calibre unknown to us.

I write here in no fanatical or adventist spirit; I speak not as a speculative theologian or an exponent of one phase of religious, wishful thinking. I speak because many know that the time is ripe and that the appeal of simple, faithful hearts has penetrated to the highest spiritual sphere and set in motion energies and forces which cannot now be stopped. The invocative cry of distressed humanity is today of such a volume and sound that—united to the wisdom and the knowledge of the Spiritual Hierarchy—it has given rise to certain activities in the Father's House. These will result in the glory of God, in the transformation of the divine will-to-good into human goodwill, and resultant peace on Earth.

A new chapter in the great book of spiritual living is about to be written; a new expansion of consciousness is an imminent happening; a fresh recognition of divine attentiveness is now possible to humanity and a revealing expectancy will prove the accuracy of the Biblical statement, "every eye shall see Him." (Rev. 1.7.) The religious livingness or spiritual history of mankind can be summarised for us by a series of recognitions—recognition of Those Who, down the ages, have constituted the Apostolic Succession, culminating for us in the great religious leaders who have come out among us since 700 B.C. and founded the great modern world faiths, and—above all else—in the Christ Himself Who embodied the perfection of God Immanent, plus awareness of God Transcendent; recognition of those major spiritual concepts of love, life and relationship which have hovered ever in the background of man's thinking and which are now on the verge of right expression; recognition of the true brotherhood of man, *based on the one divine life, working through the one soul and expressing itself through the one humanity;* recognition, therefore, of relationship both to the divine life throughout the world and to mankind itself. It is this developing spiritual attitude which will lead to right human relations and eventual world peace.

Today, another recognition is becoming possible. It is the recognition everywhere of the imminent return of Christ (if such a phrase can be true of someone Who has never left us!) and of the new spiritual opportunities which this event will make possible.

The basis for this recognition lies in the deep-seated conviction, innate in the human consciousness, that some great Teacher, some Saviour, Revealer, Lawgiver or divine Representative *must* come forth from the world of spiritual realities, because of human need and human demand. Always down the centuries, at the hour of man's greatest need and in response to his voiced demand, a divine Son of God *has* come forth and under many different names. Then the Christ came and apparently left us, with His work unfinished and His vision for mankind not yet consummated. For two thousand years it has seemed as if all His work had been blocked, frustrated, and of no avail, for the growth of the churches during the centuries is no guarantee of the spiritual success at which He aimed. It needed more than theological interpretations and the numerical growth of the world religions (including Christianity and Buddhism) to prove His world mission successfully carried forward. It all seemed impossible, necessitating three conditions; under these a test of His work could be attempted; today these three conditions are proven facts. First, as we have seen, a general planetary condition which has unfortunately (owing to man's selfishness) proved to be so catastrophic in nature that humanity has been forced to recognise the cause and source of the disaster; secondly, a spiritual awakening which would have its impulse in the deepest depths of man's consciousness and such is the case today as a result of the World War (1914-1945); thirdly, a steadily mounting invocative cry, prayer or demand, directed toward high spiritual sources, no matter by what name such sources may be called.

Today, these three conditions have been fulfilled and humanity faces renewed opportunity. The disaster which has overtaken mankind is universal and widespread; no one has escaped and all men are involved in some way or another—physically, economically or socially. The spiritual awakening of men everywhere (within or without the world faiths, and largely outside of them) is general and complete and a turning to God is to be seen on every hand. Finally, these two causes have aroused—as never before—the invocative cry of humanity; it is clearer, purer and more selfless than at any other time in human history because it is based on clearer thinking and a common distress. True religion is again emerging in the hearts of men in every land; this recognition of a divine hope and background may possibly take people back into the church and into the world faiths, but *it will most certainly take them back to God.*

Religion is the name, surely, which we give to the invocative appeal of humanity which leads to the evocative response of the Spirit of God. This Spirit works in every human heart and in all groups. It works also through the Spiritual Hierarchy of the planet. It impels the Head of the Hierarchy, the Christ, to take action and the action which He is taking will lead to His return with His disciples.

The idea of the return of Christ is a most familiar one, and the concept of the Son of God returning in response to human need has its place in the teaching of the majority of the world faiths. Ever since He apparently departed to the sphere where the faithful have put Him, little groups of these people have reasoned themselves into the belief that on such and such a date He will come back, and ever their prophecies and expectancies have been doomed to failure. He has not come. Such people have been laughed at by the crowd and rebuked by the intelligent. Their eyes have not seen Him and there has been no tangible indication of His Presence. Today, thousands know that He will come; that plans for His coming are already set on foot, but *they set no date or hour.* The time is known only to the two or three, but "in such an hour as ye think not, He will come." (Matt. XXIV.44.)

A truth hard for the orthodox thinker of any faith to accept is the fact that *Christ cannot return because He has always been here upon our Earth,* watching over the spiritual destiny of humanity; He has never left us but, in physical body and securely concealed (though not hidden), He has guided the affairs of the Spiritual Hierarchy, of His disciples and workers Who are unitedly pledged with Him to Earth service. *He can only re-appear.*

It is a spiritual fact that those who have passed from the cave of the tomb into the fullness of the resurrection life can be seen and at the same time evade the vision of the believer. Seeing and recognition are two very different things, and one of the great recognitions of mankind in the near future is the recognition that always He has been with us, sharing with us the familiar usefulness and peculiar characteristics of our civilisation and its many gifts to man.

The early signs of His approach with His disciples can already be discerned by those who note and rightly interpret the signs of the times. There is (among these signs) the coming together spiritually of those who love their fellowmen. This is in reality the organising of the outer physical army of the Lord—an army which has no weapons but those of love, of right speech and right human relations. This unknown organisation has proceeded with phenomenal speed during the aftermath of war, because humanity is sick of hate and controversy.

The general staff of the Christ is already active in the form of the New Group of World Servers; they are as potent a body of forerunners as has ever preceded a great world Figure into the arena of mankind's living. Their work and influence is already seen and felt in every land, and nothing can destroy that which they have accomplished. The spiritual and organising effect of expressed and voiced invocation has been also attempted since 1935, and the energy of the invocative cry of humanity has been directed into those channels which reach from Earth to that High Place where dwells the Christ. From there, it has been transmitted to those still higher spheres where the attention of the Lord of the World, the Ancient of Days, the Father of all, plus the Creative Energies and Living Beings Who dwell there with Him, can be focussed on humanity and those steps can be taken which will embody more rapidly the Purposes of God.

For the first time in human history, the demand of the people of the Earth is so potent and so in line with divine direction, in time and space, that the end is inevitably sure; the looked-for spiritual Representative must come forth; this time He will not come alone but will be accompanied by Those Whose lives and words will evoke recognition in every department of human thinking. The symbolic prophecies found in all the world Scriptures anent this imminent event will prove their veracity; their symbolism will nevertheless elicit re-interpretation; circumstances and happenings will not necessarily be exactly as the Scriptures would appear to indicate. For instance, He will come indeed in the "clouds of the air" (Matt. XXVI. 64), as the Christian Scriptures say, but of what great interest is that when millions come and go in the clouds, each hour of the day and of the night? I mention this as one of the outstanding prophecies and one of the most familiar; it is, however, one which means little in our modern civilisation. The fact of importance is that He will come.

The Wesak Festival has been held down the centuries in the well-known valley in the Himalayas (if the faithful would only believe it) in order:

1. To substantiate the fact of Christ's physical existence among us ever since His so-called departure.

2. To prove (on the physical plane) the factual solidarity of the Eastern and Western approaches to God. Both the Christ and the Buddha are present.

3. To form a rallying-point and a meeting-place for those who annually—in synthesis and symbolically—link up and represent the Father's House, the Kingdom of God and Humanity.

4. To demonstrate the nature of the work of Christ as the great and chosen Intermediary, standing as the Representative of the Spiritual Hierarchy and as the Leader of the New Group of World Servers. In His Person, He voices their demand for the recognition of the factual existence of the Kingdom of God here and now.

Perhaps one of the major messages for all of us who read these words is this great truth and fact of the physical Presence on Earth at this time of the Christ, of His group of disciples and executives, of Their representative activities on behalf of mankind and of Their close relationship. This relationship comes out at certain of the great spiritual festivals where the relationship demonstrated includes not only the Kingdom of God but also the Father and the Father's Home. There is the Festival of Easter, the Festival of the Buddha Who in physical Presence expresses the spiritual solidarity of our planet, and the Festival in June, peculiarly the Festival of the Christ, when He—as leader of the New Group of World Servers—employs the new Invocation on behalf of all men of goodwill in all lands; at the same time, He gathers up the inchoate and unexpressed demands of those masses who seek a new and better way of life. They want love in daily living, right human relations and an understanding of the underlying Plan.

It is these physical happenings which are of moment and not the vague hopes and promises of the theological faiths. It is the physical Presence upon our planet of such recognised spiritual figures as the Lord of the World, the Ancient of Days; the seven Spirits Who are before the throne of God; the Buddha, the spiritual leader of the East, and the Christ, the spiritual leader of the West—all of Whom are brought at this climaxing time to our attention. The vague belief in Their existence, the dreamy speculations as to Their work and Their interest in human welfare, and the unconvinced, yet hopeful, wishful thinking of believers (and also unbelievers), will soon give place to certain knowledge, to visual recognition, to provable signs of executive work and to the reorganisation (by men of unusual potency) of the political, religious, economic and social life of humanity.

All this will not come as the result of some proclamation or some stupendous planetary event which will force human beings everywhere to say: "Lo: He is there! Lo: Here are the signs of His divinity!" for that would evoke only antagonism and laughter, resistance or fanatical credulity.

It will come as a recognition of potency in leadership, through dynamic but logical changes in world affairs, and through action taken by the masses of the people from the depths of their own consciousness.

Many years ago, I indicated that the Christ would come in three ways, or rather, that the fact of His Presence could be proved in three distinctive phases.

It was pointed out then that the first move which the Christ would make would be the stimulation of the spiritual consciousness in man, the evocation of humanity's spiritual demands on a large scale and the nurturing—on a worldwide scale—of the Christ consciousness in the human heart. This has already been done and with most effective results. Of the factual nature of this process, the vociferous demands of men of goodwill, of welfare workers and of those pledged to international cooperation, to the relief of the world distress and to the establishment of right human relations, are the undeniable expression. That phase of the preparatory work which is indicative of His coming has now reached a stage where nothing can arrest its progress or slow down its momentum. In spite of appearances, this uprising of the Christ consciousness has been successful and what may appear as reverse activity is of no importance in the long run, but is only of a temporary nature.

The second indicated move of the Hierarchy would be the impressing of the minds of enlightened men everywhere by spiritual ideas embodying the new truths, by the "descent" (if I may so call it) of the new concepts which will govern human living and by the overshadowing of all world disciples and the New Group of World Servers by the Christ Himself. This planned move of the Hierarchy is progressing well; men and women everywhere and in every department of life are enunciating those new truths which should in the future guide human living; they are building those new organisations, movements and groups—large or small—which will familiarise the mass of men with the reality of the need and the mode of meeting it. This they are doing because they are driven thereto by the warmth of their hearts and by their loving response to human distress; without formulating it thus to themselves, they are, nevertheless, working to bring into visibility the Kingdom of God on Earth. No denial of these facts is possible, in view of the multiplicity of organisations, books and speeches.

Thirdly, we are told that Christ might come in Person and walk among men as He did before. This has not yet taken place but plans are being laid which will enable Him to do so. Those plans do not involve the birth of some nice child in some nice home on Earth; they will not produce the wild claims and the credulous recognition of the well-meaning and the unintelligent as is so frequently the case today, nor will someone appear and say: "This is the Christ. He is here or He is there." I would point out to you, however, that the widespread appearance of such tales and claims, though undesirable, misleading and wrong, nevertheless demonstrates human expectancy of the imminence of His coming. Belief in His coming is basic in the human consciousness. How He will come and in what manner is not yet stated. The exact moment has not yet arrived nor has the method of His appearance been determined. The factual nature of the two earlier and preparatory moves, already made by the Hierarchy under His direction, is the guarantee that He will come and that when He does, mankind will be ready.

Let us summarise certain aspects of the work He set in motion two thousand years ago, because they hold the clue to His future work. Some of it is well known to you, for it has been emphasised by the world faiths and particularly by teachers of the Christian faith. But all of them have made His work appear difficult for man to grasp, and the undue emphasis laid upon His divinity (an emphasis which He Himself never made) has made it appear that He and He only and no one else could possibly do the same works. Theologians have forgotten that He Himself stated that "greater things shall ye do, because I go unto my Father." (John XIV. 12.) He here indicates that this passing to the Father's House would result in such an inflow of spiritual strength, insight and creative accomplishment for man, that their deeds would surpass His; because of the distortion of His teaching and its remote relation to man, we have not yet done those "greater things." Some day, we assuredly will and—along certain lines—we already have. Let me relate some of the things He did which we can do, and which He will aid.

1. For the first time in human history, the love of God was embodied in a man and Christ inaugurated the era of love. That expression of divine love is still in the

making; the world is not yet full of love and few there are who understand the true meaning of the word. But—speaking symbolically—when the United Nations has emerged into factual and actual power, the welfare of the world will then be assured. What is that welfare but love in action? What is international cooperation but love on a world scale? Those are the things which the love of God in Christ expressed and those are the things which we are working here today to bring into being. We are attempting to do it on a vast scale and this in spite of opposition—an opposition which can only temporarily succeed, such is the potency of the awakened spirit of man. These are the things which the Hierarchy, in its already successful procedures, is aiding and will continue to aid.

2. Christ taught also that the Kingdom of God was on Earth and told us to seek that Kingdom first and let all things be of secondary importance for its sake. That Kingdom has ever been with us, composed of all those who down the ages, have sought spiritual goals, liberated themselves from the limitations of the physical body, emotional controls and the obstructive mind. Its citizens are those who today (unknown to the majority) live in physical bodies, work for the welfare of humanity, use love instead of emotion as their general technique, and compose that great body of "illumined Minds" which guides the destiny of the world. The Kingdom of God is not something which will descend on Earth when man is good enough! It is something which is functioning efficiently today and demanding recognition. It is an organised body which is already evoking recognition from those people who do seek first the Kingdom of God, and discover thereby that the Kingdom they seek is already here. Christ and His disciples are known by many to be

physically present on Earth and the Kingdom which They rule, with its laws and modes of activity, is familiar to many and has been throughout the centuries.

Christ is the world Healer and Saviour. He works because He is the embodied soul of all Reality. He works today, as He worked in Palestine two thousand years ago, through groups. There He worked through the three beloved disciples, through the twelve apostles, through the chosen seventy, and the interested five hundred. . . . Now He works through His Masters and Their groups, and thereby greatly intensifies His efforts. He can and will work through all groups just insofar as they fit themselves for planned service, for the distribution of love, and come into conscious alignment with the great potency of the inner groups.

Those groups who have always proclaimed the physical Presence of the Christ have so distorted the teaching by dogmatic assertions on unimportant details and by ridiculous claims that they have evoked little recognition of the underlying truth, nor have they portrayed a kingdom which is attractive. That Kingdom exists but is not a place of disciplines or golden harps, peopled by unintelligent fanatics, but a field of service and a place where every man has full scope for the exercise of his divinity in human service.

3. At the Transfiguration, Christ revealed the glory which is innate in all men. The triple lower nature—physical, emotional and mental—is there shown as prostrate before the glory which was revealed. In that moment, wherein Christ Immanent was in incarnation, wherein humanity was represented by the three apostles, a voice came from the Father's Home in recognition of the revealed divinity and the Sonship of the Transfigured Christ. On this innate divinity, upon this recognised

Sonship, is the brotherhood of all men based—one life, one glory which shall be revealed, and one divine relationship. Today, on a large scale (even when by-passing the implications of divinity), the glory of man and his fundamental relationships are already a fact in the human consciousness. Accompanying those characteristics which as yet remain deplorable and which would appear to negate all claims to divinity, is the wonder of man's achievement, of his triumph over nature. The glory of scientific attainment and the magnificent evidence of creative art—both modern and ancient—leave no room to question man's divinity. Here then are the "greater things" of which Christ spoke and here again is the triumph of the Christ within the human heart.

Why this triumph of the Christ consciousness must always be spoken of in terms of religion, of church-going and of orthodox belief is one of the incredible triumphs of the forces of evil. To be a citizen of the Kingdom of God does not mean that one must necessarily be a member of some one of the orthodox churches. The divine Christ in the human heart can be expressed in many different departments of human living—in politics, in the arts, in economic expression and in true social living, in science and in religion. It might be wise here to remember that the only time it is recorded that Christ (as an adult) visited the Temple of the Jews, He created a disturbance! Humanity is passing from glory to glory and, in the long panorama of history, this is strikingly observable. That glory is today revealed in every department of human activity, and the Transfiguration of those who are on the crest of the human wave of civilisation is very close at hand.

4. Finally, in the triumph of the Crucifixion or (as it is more accurately called in the East) the Great Renun-

ciation, Christ, for the first time, anchored on Earth a tenuous thread of the divine Will as it issued from the Father's House (Shamballa), passed into the understanding custody of the Kingdom of God and, through the medium of the Christ, was brought to the attention of mankind. Through the instrumentality of certain great Sons of God, the three divine aspects or characteristics of the divine Trinity—will, love and intelligence—have become a part of human thinking and aspiration. Christians are apt to forget that the crisis in the final hours of the Christ was not that spent upon the Cross, but those spent in the Garden of Gethsemane. Then His will —in agony and almost despair—was submerged in that of the Father. "Father," He said, "not My will but Thine be done." (Luke XXII. 42.)

Something new, yet planned for from the very depth of time, happened then in that quiet garden; Christ, representing mankind, anchored or established the Father's Will on Earth and made it possible for intelligent humanity to carry it out. Hitherto, that Will had been known in the Father's House; it had been recognised and adapted to world need by the Spiritual Hierarchy, working under the Christ, and thus took shape as the divine Plan. Today, because of what Christ did in His moment of crisis hundreds of years ago, humanity can add its efforts to the working out of that Plan. The will-to-good of the Father's House can become the goodwill of the Kingdom of God and be transformed into right human relations by intelligent humanity. Thus the direct line or thread of God's will reaches now from the highest place to the lowest point, and can in due time become a cable of ascension for the sons of men and of descent for the loving, living spirit of God.

Let us forget distance, remoteness and vagueness and realise that we are talking of exact and literal happenings on our planet. We are dealing with recognitions and occurrences and with factual events which are the conscious possession of many. *The Christ of history and the Christ in the human heart are planetary facts.*

There is one aspect of this return of the Christ which is never touched upon and to which no reference is ever made. It is the factor of what this coming out again among men, this return to outer everyday activity will mean to the Christ as He faces it. How will He feel when the hour of His appearance arrives?

There is a great initiation spoken of in *The New Testament* to which we have given the name of the Ascension. Of it we know nothing. Only a few items of information are brought to us in the Gospel story; the fact of the mountain top, of attendant watchers, and of the words of Christ, assuring them that He was not leaving them. Then a cloud received Him out of their sight. (Acts I. 9.) There were none present who could go further with Him. Their consciousness could not penetrate to the place where He had chosen to go; they even misinterpreted His words and only in a vague and mystical sense has humanity ever understood His disappearance, or the significance of His persistent but unobserved Presence. The watchers were assured by two of the Knowers of God Who were also present that He would come again in like manner. He ascended. The cloud received Him; today the clouds which cover our planet are waiting to reveal Him.

He is now waiting to descend. This descent into our unhappy world of men can present Him with no alluring picture. From the quiet mountain retreat where He has waited, guided and watched over humanity and where

He has trained His disciples, initiates and the New Group of World Servers, He must come forth and take His place prominently on the world stage; take His part in the great drama which is there being played. This time, He will play His part, not in obscurity as He previously did but before the eyes of the entire world. Because of the smallness of our little planet, and because of the prevalence of the radio, of television and the rapidity of communication, His part will be watched by all and the prospect must surely, for Him, hold certain horror, must present its tests and major adjustments, plus painful and unavoidable experience. He does not come as the omnipotent God of man's ignorant creation, but as the Christ, the Founder of the Kingdom of God on Earth, to complete the work He started, and again to demonstrate divinity in far more difficult circumstances.

The Christ suffers, however, far more from those in His Own household than from those in the outer world; His work is more impeded by the advanced aspirant than by the intelligent thinker. It was not the cruelty of the outer world of men which caused the depths of sorrow to the Christ; it was His Own disciples, plus the massed sorrow—spread over the entire cycle of living—past, present and future—of humanity.

He comes to correct the mistakes and the misrepresentations of those who have dared to interpret His simple words in terms of their own ignorance, and to recognise those whose faithful service has made His return possible. He too is facing a major test, preparatory to a great initiation and when He has passed the test and fulfilled His task, He will pass to a still more exalted position in the Father's House or to some distant place of service where only the most exalted can follow Him;

His present position will then be taken by the One Whom He has prepared and trained.

But before all this can happen, He must again enter the public arena, play His part in world affairs, and prove the scope of His mission. He will gather round Him, in the flesh, His chosen associates and advisors; these will not be the ones who gathered around in those earlier simpler days but those members of our human family who today recognise Him and are preparing to work with Him as far as in them lies. It is a different world to which He is now planning to return and this is largely due to the intellectual development of the mass of men. This presents Him with stupendous difficulties, for the intellects of men must now be reached and not just their hearts (as in the earlier days) if the Will of God is to be intelligently carried out on Earth. His major task is surely the establishing of right human relations in every department of human living. I would ask you to use your imagination and endeavour to think out what must be the implications of the task which confronts Him; I would ask you to ponder on the difficulties which He must inevitably face—the difficulty, above all, of mass intellectual wrong emphasis.

He, the Representative of the love of God, is asked to work again in the world arena wherein His earlier message has been negated, forgotten or misinterpreted for two thousand years, and wherein hate and separativeness have distinguished all men everywhere. This will plunge Him into a foreign atmosphere and into a situation wherein all His divine resources will be needed, and will have to be tried out to the uttermost. The generally accepted idea that He will return as a triumphant warrior, omnipotent and irresistible, has surely no basis in fact. That He will ultimately lead His people, humanity, into Jerusalem is a fact, founded on a secure foundation, but it will not be into a Jewish city called Jerusalem but into "the place of peace" (as the word "Jerusalem" means). A careful consideration of the world situation today and a dedicated use of the imagination will reveal to the sincere thinker how appalling is the task which He has undertaken. But He has again "set His face to go to Jerusalem." (Luke IX.51.) He will re-appear and guide mankind into a civilisation and a state of consciousness in which right human relations and worldwide cooperation for the good of all will be the universal keynote. He will—through the New Group of World Servers and the men of goodwill—complete His association with the Will of God (His Father's business) in such a manner that the eternal will-to-good will be translated by humanity into goodwill and right relations. Then His task will be done; He will be free again to leave us, but this time not to return but to leave the world of men in the hands of that great spiritual Server Who will be the new Head of the Hierarchy, the Church Invisible.

The question now arises: In what way can we be of service? How can we aid during this preparatory stage?

What the members of the Spiritual Hierarchy are doing is much indeed; those disciples who are in conscious touch with the Masters of the Wisdom—or, if you prefer the term, with the senior disciples of the Christ—are working day and night in order to establish such confidence, correct attitudes and an understanding of the divine spiritual "push" or enterprise that His way will be made easier. They and their groups of lesser disciples, aspirants and students of the realities stand unitedly behind the Christ and can thus enable Him to accomplish His purpose. Their major realisation is that of a cyclic crisis in the spiritual life of our planet; it is one which has been anticipated in the Father's House (Shamballa) for thousands of years. They have registered the fact that, for the first time in human history, all the three spiritual centres or groups through which God works are unitedly focussed on the same objective. Shamballa, the Spiritual Hierarchy and Humanity (the Father's House, the Kingdom of God and the World of Men) are all striving in one vast movement for an intensification of the Light of the World. This Light will irradiate (in a fashion unknown before) not only the Father's House, which is the source of all our planetary light but also the spiritual centre from which have come all those Teachers and World Saviours Who have stood before men and said, as did Hermes, the Buddha and the Christ: "I am the Light of the World." This light will now flood the world of men, bringing illumination to men's minds and light into the dark places of human living.

It is light and—above all else—"life more abundantly" which Christ will bring, and until He brings it we know not what it signifies; we cannot realise the revelation which this will entail and the new possibilities which will open up before us. But through Him, light and life are on their way, to be interpreted and applied in terms of goodwill and of right human relations. For this the Spiritual Hierarchy is preparing. This time the Christ will not come alone for His co-workers will come with Him. His experience and Theirs will be the reverse of the previous one, for this time every eye will see Him, every ear will hear Him and every mind will pass judgment upon Him.

We can freely aid in the reconstruction work which the Christ proposes, if we will familiarise ourselves and all men whom we can contact with the following facts:

1. That the reappearance of Christ is imminent.

2. That the Christ, immanent in every human heart, can be evoked in recognition of His appearance.

3. That the circumstances of His return are only symbolically related in the world Scriptures; this may produce a vital change in the preconceived ideas of humanity.

4. That the major required preparation is a world at peace; however, that peace must be based on an educated goodwill, which will lead inevitably to right human relations, and, therefore, to the establishment (figuratively speaking) of lines of light between nation and nation, religion and religion, group and group and man and man.

If we can succeed in presenting these four ideas to the world at large, and thus in overcoming the intelligent criticism that all that is said is too vague, prophetic, and visionary, we shall have done much. It is possible surely that the ancient truism that "the mind is the slayer of the real" may be fundamentally true where the mass of humanity is concerned and that the purely intellectual approach (which rejects the vision and refuses to accept the unprovable) may be far more at fault than the anticipation of the Knowers of God and the expectant multitude.

The intelligence of divinity is vested in the Spiritual Hierarchy, and that Hierarchy is today composed of Those Who have united in Themselves both the intellect and the intuition, the practical and the apparently impractical, the factual way of life and way of the man who sees a vision. There are also people who must be found in the market place of daily life; these are the people who must be trained in the divine recognitions which are essentially physical plane responses to the newer expansions of consciousness. The Christ Who will return will not be like the Christ Who (apparently) departed. He will not be a "man of sorrows"; He will not be a silent pensive figure; He will be the enunciator of spiritual statements which will not necessitate interpretation and receive the wrong interpretation, because He will be present to indicate the true meaning.

He has been for two thousand years the supreme Head of the Church Invisible, the Spiritual Hierarchy, composed of disciples of all faiths. He recognises and loves those who are not Christian but who retain their allegiance to Their Founders—the Buddha, Mohammed and others. He cares not what the faith is if the objective is love of God and of humanity. If men look for the Christ Who left His disciples centuries ago, they will fail to recognise the Christ Who is in process of returning. The Christ has no religious barriers in His consciousness. It matters not to Him of what faith a man may call himself.

The Son of God is on His way and He cometh not alone. His advance guard is already here and the Plan which they must follow is already made and clear. Let recognition be the aim.

CHAPTER FOUR

THE WORK OF THE CHRIST TODAY AND IN THE FUTURE

WE have seen that the doctrine of great Appearances and of the coming of Avatars or World Teachers or Saviours underlies all the world religions. Through Them, the continuity of revelation is implemented and humanity is enabled, each successive age, to take its next step forward along the Path of Evolution closer to God and that divine Centre in which the will of the One "in Whom we live and move and have our being" (as St. Paul expressed it in Acts XVII.28) is focussed, understood and directed. We have touched upon the mission of two of these Avatars—the Buddha, the Messenger of Light for the East, and the Christ, the Messenger of Love for the West—and Their work for the entire world; we have also considered the unique opportunity with which Christ is today faced and the response He made in 1945 when He signified His intention to reappear and gave the great Invocation to us as an aid in the preparatory work with which we are immediately confronted. It would seem appropriate at this point to consider the nature of the work which He will do and also the teaching which He will probably give. The fact of the continuity of the revelation and teaching given down the ages entitles us to a wise consideration and spiritual speculation upon the probable lines which His work will take.

Over the years, much has been given out from many sources, schools of thought and churches about the Christ, the situation which He faces and the probabilities as to His reappearance. Disciples, aspirants, and men of goodwill have done much already to prepare the world for His so-called return. Today, the East and the West stand equally expectant. As we approach the theme of His work, it is essential that we remember that the Eastern Teacher embodied in Himself the Wisdom of God, of which human intelligence (the third aspect of divinity) is an expression; that through Christ, the second divine aspect was revealed in its perfection; and in Him two aspects, therefore, light and love, received full expression. It remains now for the highest of the divine aspects, the Will of God, to receive embodiment and for this the Christ is preparing. The continuity of revelation may not stop; and upon what other expressions of the divine nature may still later be revealed it is needless for us to speculate.

The uniqueness of the impending mission of the Christ and the uniqueness of His opportunity consist in the fact that He is able—in Himself—to give expression to two divine energies: the energy of love and the energy of will, the magnetic potency of love and the dynamic effectiveness of the divine will. Never before, in the long long history of humanity, has such a revelation been possible.

The work and the teaching of the Christ will be hard for the Christian world to accept, though easier of assimilation in the East. Nevertheless, some hard blow or some difficult presentation of the truth is badly needed if the Christian world is to be awakened, and if Christian people are to recognise their place within a worldwide divine revelation and see Christ as representing all the faiths and taking His rightful place as World Teacher. He is the *World* Teacher and not a Christian teacher. He Himself told us that He had other folds and to them He has meant

THE WORK OF THE CHRIST

as much as He has meant to the orthodox Christian. They may not call Him Christ, but they have their own name for Him and follow Him as truly and faithfully as their Western brethren.

Let us look for a moment at the erroneous interpretations given to the Gospel story. The symbolism of that Gospel story—an ancient story-presentation often presented down the ages, prior to the coming of the Christ in Palestine—has been twisted and distorted by theologians until the crystalline purity of the early teaching and the unique simplicity of the Christ have disappeared in a travesty of errors and in a mummery of ritual, money and human ambitions. Christ is pictured today as having been born in an unnatural manner, as having taught and preached for three years and then as having been crucified and eventually resurrected, leaving humanity in order to "sit on the right hand of God," in austere and distant pomp. Likewise, all the other approaches to God by any other people, at any time and in any country, are regarded by the orthodox Christian as wrong approaches, as being practiced by so-called "heathen," and as requiring Christian interference. Every possible effort has been made to force orthodox Christianity on those who accept the inspiration and the teachings of the Buddha or of others who have been responsible for preserving the divine continuity of revelation. The emphasis has been, as we all well know, upon the "blood sacrifice of the Christ" upon the Cross and upon a salvation dependent upon the recognition and acceptance of that sacrifice. The vicarious at-one-ment has been substituted for the reliance which Christ Himself enjoined us to place upon our own divinity; the Church of Christ has made itself famous and futile (as the world war proved) for its narrow creed, its wrong emphases, its clerical pomp, its spurious authority, its material riches and its presentation of a dead Christ. His resurrection is accepted, but the major appeal of the churches has been upon His death.

Christ has been for two thousand years a silent, passive Figure, hidden behind a multitude of words written by a multitude of men (commentators and preachers). The church has pointed us to the dying Christ upon the Cross and not to the living, working, active, present Christ Who has been with us in bodily Presence (according to His promise) for twenty centuries.

Let us, therefore, endeavour to get a truer picture of Christ's activities and life and—consequently—of our future hope. Let us try and realise the ever-present yet divine Person, laying His plans for the future helping of humanity, assessing His resources, influencing His disciples and organising the details which will attend His reappearance. We need to awaken faith in the *factual* nature of divine revelation, and galvanise the church of Christ into a truer appreciation of Him and of His work. It is the living, acting, thinking Christ with whom we must deal, remembering always that *the Gospel story is eternally true* and only needs re-interpreting in the light of its place in the long succession of divine revelations. His Mission on earth two thousand years ago is a part of that continuity and is not an extraordinary story, having no relation to the past, emphasising a period of only 33 years and presenting no clear hope for the future.

What is the hope held out today by the orthodox and unimaginative theologians? That at some distant date, known only to the inscrutable will of God the Father, Christ will issue forth from His seat at the right hand of God, and (followed by His angels and by the Church invisible) descending upon the clouds of Heaven, to the sound of a trumpet, He will make an appearance in

THE WORK OF THE CHRIST

Jerusalem. The battle raging at that time will then end, and He will enter the city of Jerusalem to rule for one thousand years. During this millennium, Satan or the principle of evil will be bound or imprisoned, and there will be a new heaven and new earth. Further than that, we are told nothing; humanity hopes for so much more that the picture presented does not intrigue them.

Behind this portrayal, if rightly interpreted, stands the human, the loving and the divine Presence of the Christ, embodying divine love and wielding divine power, directing His Church and establishing the Kingdom of God on Earth. What is this church of Christ? It is constituted of the sumtotal of all those in whom the life of Christ or the Christ-consciousness is to be found or is in process of finding expression; it is the aggregation of all who love their fellowmen, because to love one's fellowmen is the divine faculty which makes us full members of Christ's community. It is not the accepting of any historical fact or theological creed which places us en rapport with Christ. The citizens of the Kingdom of God are all those who are deliberately seeking the light and attempting (through self-imposed discipline) to stand before the One Initiator; this worldwide group (whether in the body or out of it) accepts the teaching that "the sons of men are one"; they know that divine revelation is continuous and ever new, and that the divine Plan is working itself out on Earth.

There are those today on Earth who know that through the instrumentality, the inspiration and the instruction of those sons of men who have wrought out their divinity in the crucible of daily human living the Kingdom of God will come into being; these Knowers now work actively, under the direct impression of the Christ, in leading humanity from darkness to light and from death to immortality.

These are the great underlying truths which are distinctive of the Christ, of the Buddha, and of the Church of God, as it expresses itself in the East and in the West; these are the only truths which matter. In the future, the eyes of humanity will be fixed upon Christ and not upon any such manmade institutions as the Church and its dignitaries; Christ will be seen as He is in reality, working through His disciples, through the Masters of the Wisdom and through His followers who toil unseen (and usually unrecognised) behind world affairs. The sphere of His activity will be known to be the human heart and also the crowded market places of the world, but not some stone edifice and not the pomp and ceremony of any ecclesiastical headquarters.

Our study of the future work of the Christ is necessarily based upon three assumptions:

1. That the reappearance of the Christ is inevitable and assured.

2. That He is today and has been actively working—through the medium of the spiritual Hierarchy of our planet, of which He is the Head—for the welfare of humanity.

3. That certain teachings will be given and certain energies will be released by Him in the routine of His work and coming. People are apt to forget that the coming of the Christ necessitates a period of intensive preparation by Him; He, too, works under law and is subject to control from various sources—just as are all human beings, but in a much lesser degree.

His reappearance is conditioned and determined by the reaction of humanity itself; by that reaction He must abide. His work is subject also to certain phases of *spir-*

itual and cyclic timing and to impressions from sources to be found on higher levels than those upon which He normally works. Just as human affairs have effects upon His action, so great "determinations" and "profound settlements within the will of God" also have their effects. The human side or nature of the Christ, perfected and sensitive, responds to the invocation and to the appeal of men; His divine side or nature is equally responsive to the impact of energies, issuing from "the centre where the will of God is known." Between these two, He has to make adjustment and bring about right timing. The bringing of good out of human so-called evil is no easy task; the vision of the Christ is so vast and His grasp of the Law of Cause and Effect, of Action and Reaction is such that the arriving at right decision as to activity and time is no simple one. Human beings are apt to look at all that happens, or that could happen, from the purely human and immediate angle; they have little understanding of the problems, decisions and implications with which Christ is today faced. In these, His pledged disciples share. Their task is to develop "the mind that is in Christ" and as they do so, they will help make clear the way for "the coming of His feet," as the Bible puts it (Heb. XII.13). Seeing life and events in the light of the spiritual values, as He does, will facilitate the giving out of the new teaching and will provide the skeleton structure of the new world religion, thus giving us a fresh view of divine intention and a living insight into the minds of Those Who implement the divine will and are the engineers of humanity's future. Let us, therefore, try and appreciate not only the opportunity which Christ has to help us (which is the usual presentation), but let us look also at the crises and problems with which He is confronted as He faces the work which He must do.

I. *The Crises of the Christ*

In the life of every disciple, particularly of those who face certain great expansions of consciousness, a *point of crisis* will come about. In that point of crisis, decisions are voluntarily or involuntarily made; having made them, the disciple then stands at a *point of tension,* with the decision behind him and the next step to be taken becoming clearer to his mental perception, and influencing his attitude to the future. When the work is done in the period of tension, then there comes what we might call the *point of emergence.* This is both an emergence from and also an emergence into a field of experience.

The Christ Himself is no exception to this threefold experience and—in order that we may understand more fully—let us apply these three phrases (inappropriate as they basically are) to the actions and the reactions of the Christ.

There is no crisis for Him in the sense that crises exist for us; there is no strain or stress attached to His point of tension; the parallel is, however, good enough to convey something to you of what has transpired within that state of awareness which distinguishes the spiritual Hierarchy; to this state of consciousness we can give the name of "spiritual perception," in contradistinction to the mental perception which is the human counterpart. It must be remembered that the point of crisis, producing the point of tension to which the Christ may be regarded as voluntarily subjecting Himself is a hierarchical matter or event, because the entire Hierarchy is involved in the crisis. The reason for this is simple: the Christ and His workers know only the experience of *group consciousness.* A separative participation and attitude is unknown to

THE WORK OF THE CHRIST

Them, for Their state of awareness is inclusive and in no way exclusive.

Using, therefore, human terminology in order to interpret the divine reactions of the Christ and His disciples, it must be realised that the point of crisis which is responsible for hierarchical tension and for the eventual appearance or the emergence of the Christ, lies behind the Christ; it is in the field of long past experience. The consequent point of tension is now controlling the affairs of the spiritual Hierarchy and its many groups of workers. The "point of decision," as it is called in all hierarchical circles, was reached during the period between the Full Moon of June, 1936, and the Full Moon of June, 1945. The point of decision covered, therefore, nine years (a relatively brief time); it resulted in the decision arrived at by the Christ to re-appear or return to visible Presence on Earth as soon as possible, and considerably earlier than had been planned.

This decision was necessarily made in consultation with the Lord of the World, the "Ancient of Days" of *The Old Testament,* and the "One in Whom we live and move and have our being" of *The New Testament.* He is the Custodian of the Will of God. It was also made with the full understanding and cooperation of the Masters and the senior initiates. This was inevitably so, because Their participation and help were imperative. They also necessarily had to be with Him in thought, and cooperating mentally, because His reappearance connotes a great hierarchical approach to humanity and a great spiritual event.

The decision was, nevertheless, the decision of the Christ and marked not only a point of crisis in His experience but a point of climax in His expression of divinity. With all reverence and within the bounds of our human understanding, it must be remembered that there is nothing static in the entire evolutionary process of our planet or of the cosmos; there is naught but process and progress, a moving on, an increasing attainment and a mounting achievement. To this great law of the universe, even the Christ Himself is subject. In all reverence again, let it here be pointed out that He too has moved on in His experience of divinity and is (if it may be so expressed) closer to the Father and to the One Universal Life than ever before. His comprehension and His apprehension of the Will of God is deeper and His fulfilment of that Will is more in line with the divine Purpose than it was in Palestine two thousand years ago. There has necessarily been (on the part of Christ) a growing perception of the intention of the divine Mind, as it is embodied in that Identity to Whom we give the name of *God*.

No longer need Christ, in agony say, "Father, not my will but Thine be done"; He has today no personal will but only the will of His Father animates Him and the ability to make decisions which are a full expression of that divine Will. It is difficult to express His achievement in other words. Commentators have sought to explain away and gloss over the Gethsemane experience of the Christ, and to attribute what appears as weakness to an upsurging of Christ's humanity and, consequently, to a temporary submergence of His divine nature. They have been forced into this position because of the prevalent theological dictum as to Christ's divine perfection—an absolute, sovereign and ultimate perfection to which He Himself never made the slightest claim. He is today nearer that perfection than He ever was when before on Earth. It was this divine unfoldment which made it possible for Him to make right choice, not only for Him-

THE WORK OF THE CHRIST

self but also for the spiritual Hierarchy, during the years of decision, prior to June, 1945.

Under the divine will, He had to reappear on Earth in visible Presence. He had to preside over the materialisation of the Kingdom of God on Earth, and He had to re-institute the Mysteries of Initiation in such a form that they would prove the basis of the new world religion. Above all, He had to reveal the nature of the will of God. That will is often regarded as a power by means of which things are done, situations are brought about, activities are instituted and plans are worked out, and often ruthlessly worked out. This general definition is the easiest for men to formulate, because it is understood by them in terms of their own self-will, the will to individual self-betterment. This type of will is selfish and misunderstood at first, but tends eventually to selflessness, as evolution carries out its beneficent task. Then the will is interpreted in terms of the hierarchical plan and the effort of the individual man becomes that of negating his original self-will, and seeking then to merge his will with that of the group—the group being itself an aspect of hierarchical effort. This is a great step onward in orientation and will lead eventually to a change in consciousness.

It is at this stage that most aspirants today find themselves. However, the will is in reality something very different to these expressions of it which exist in the human consciousness as men attempt to interpret the divine Will in terms of their present point in evolution. The clue to understanding is to be found in the words, "blotting out all form." When the lure of substance is overcome and desire dies, then the attractive power of the soul becomes dominant, and the emphasis (so long laid upon individual form and individual living and activity) gives place to group form and group purpose. Then the attractive power of the Hierarchy and of the Masters' groups of disciples supersedes the lower attractions and the lesser focal points of interest. When these then assume their rightful place in consciousness, then the dynamic pull of the Will Aspect of divinity can be felt—entirely unrelated to form or forms, or to groups or a group.

In the light of the Will of God, Christ made certain basic decisions and determined to carry them out in the relatively immediate future—the exact date of His coming being known only to Him and a few of His senior workers; yet all of these future events lie hid in a certain fundamental decision of humanity itself. This decision is being arrived at through certain new trends in human thinking, and will be the result of a subjective human reaction to the decision already arrived at by the Christ and the spiritual Hierarchy, the Church invisible.

The motivation for this reappearance is complete and settled. It is clearly perceived by the Christ. The work initiated by Him two thousand years ago must be completed; the new world religion must be inaugurated; the needs of a demanding, invocative humanity cannot be ignored; those steps which precede a stupendous hierarchical initiation in which the Christ is the leading Participant must be taken; the events which are symptomatic of the "time of the end" may not be delayed.

If one may venture to speak in such terms (reverent and symbolical), the reward accorded to the Christ, as He announced His decision as final and irrevocable, was the permission or rather the right to use a certain great Invocation—never before granted—and to use it in two ways:

THE WORK OF THE CHRIST

1. As a hierarchical invocation, directed towards the "centre where the will of God is known."
2. As a world prayer, expressed in such phraseology that all humanity could intelligently use it.

The right to use certain great Words of Power or "Stanzas of Direction" is never lightly accorded. The decision of Christ to appear again among men, bringing His disciples with Him, drew forth this permission from the Lord of the World, the Ancient of Days.

After this climaxing point of spiritual crisis and its consequent decision, a point of tension was reached and it is in this state of spiritual tension that the Church invisible is now working and planning, swinging the disciples of the Christ, active on Earth, into the same condition of spiritual tension. The success of Christ's return to visible Presence, as well as other factors (related to His reappearance), are dependent upon happenings and contacts which are now taking place within this period of tension. In any point of tension—no matter what the time factor may be—energy is being generated, held for future use, and focussed in such a manner or condition that its force can be directed wherever needed and whenever called for. This is necessarily a statement hard to understand. A point of tension is, symbolically, a storehouse of power. Today the energies which will be uniquely distinctive of the Kingdom of God are gathering momentum and assuming direction through the agency of the Masters of the Wisdom, in cooperation with the will of Christ.

Whilst this energy has been accumulating or mounting in potency ever since the Full Moon of June 1945, three events of great moment in the living experience of Christ (and, therefore, of the Hierarchy) have taken place and their effects are in process of consolidation. I can only make reference to them, for it is not possible to prove the factual nature of what is here said; only possibility, probability and the Law of Correspondences can indicate the rightness of these events. Their effects will be noted, especially after the moment of emergence. These three events can be described as follows:

1. *The Spirit of Peace* descended upon Christ. *The New Testament* bears witness to a somewhat similar event when, at the Baptism, we read that "he saw the Spirit of God, descending like a dove and alighting upon Him." (St. Matt. III.16.) This Spirit is a Being of tremendous cosmic potency and is today overshadowing the Christ in much the same manner as Christ (two thousand years ago) overshadowed or worked through the Master Jesus. This Spirit of Peace is not the sumtotal of an emotional and static calm, bringing to an end the turmoil on the Earth and instituting an era of peace. He is, in a mysterious sense, the Spirit of Equilibrium; He works with the Law of Action and Reaction and the inevitability of His activity will be recognised. His work will demonstrate in two ways—fully when the Christ appears among men and slowly and gradually until that time:

   a. The chaos, turmoil, emotional disturbance and mental unbalance found in the world today will be (under this Law) balanced by a corresponding cycle of calm, emotional quiet and mental poise, thus releasing humanity into a new phase and experience of freedom. The adjusted peace will be commensurate to the experienced disturbance.
   b. The hate which is so dominant in the world today will—through the life of the Spirit of Peace, working through the Christ, the Embodiment of the

love of God—be balanced by an expressed goodwill. The guarantee of the appearance of that goodwill is the excessive expression of hate—a hate which has been slowly mounting in the minds of men since the beginning of the 19th century, and which is reaching a new high at this time. A proportionate measure of the energy of love will demonstrate later as the result of the activity of the Spirit of Peace, working through the Prince of Peace, as Christ has sometimes been called. (Is. IX.6.)

This spiritual Being will not descend from the high place whereon He works and from whence His energy is directed, but the Christ will act and serve as the channel for His directed potency. The inflow of His divine energy (extra-planetary energy) is destined to bring peace eventually upon Earth, through the expression of goodwill. This goodwill will bring about right human relations. Humanity registered (unconsciously, of course) the first impact of this energy in May, 1936, and again in June, 1945.

2. The evolutionary force to which we give the name "the Christ consciousness" (a term largely used by the metaphysical groups in the world today) focussed itself in the person of the Christ in a manner hitherto unknown. This is the potency, latent in every human heart which was described by St. Paul as "Christ in you, the hope of glory" (Col. I.27), and is that which, under evolutionary law, brings a man eventually into the Kingdom of God and "unto the measure of the stature of the fulness of Christ." (Eph. IV.13.) Of this potency and glory, Christ has ever been the symbol. During the

present period of hierarchical tension and as a result of His decision to reappear, Christ became the Embodiment of this energy and thus entered into a closer relation to humanity. Other great Sons of God are channels for this energy in relation to the subhuman kingdoms, but the Christ holds a unique place in relation to humanity. To express the idea symbolically, this energy creates a living bridge from the human kingdom to the Kingdom of God, from the fourth kingdom in nature to the fifth. The Christ is the custodian of this energy, but only temporarily and for the period of this human crisis. He can, because of this, stimulate the responsive factor in the hearts of men, enabling them to recognise and know Him for Who and what He is, when He reappears. This channelling of energy began at the close of the world war and is still going on; it is responsible for the trend towards betterment everywhere to be sensed, for the growth of the principle of sharing, and for the undeniable soundness of men's hearts and thinking today—the soundness of the masses (when informed), far more than of their leaders.

3. As you are well aware, human history has been essentially the history of great spiritual Messengers Who —from time to time, in the hours of human crisis—have come forth from the secret place of the Most High to aid, inspire, reveal, lead and direct. It is the history of the presentation of ideas, brought to the attention of humanity and gradually developed into civilisations and cultures. Such is the urgency of human need at this time, and such is the opportunity, that one such Son of God is— during this cycle of tension—seeking to cooperate with the Christ. As a result of Christ's decision and His "spiritual fusion" with the Will of God, the Avatar of Synthesis has become, for the time being, His close Associate.

THE WORK OF THE CHRIST

This is an event of supreme and planetary importance. His relationship and planned help date from the time of the pronouncing of the great Invocation and its use by men everywhere. Owing to the stupendous task confronting Christ, the Avatar of Synthesis will fortify Him, and He will be buttressed by this "Silent Avatar" Who (to speak symbolically) will "keep His eye upon Him, His hand beneath Him and His heart in unison with His."

This Being is closely related to the Will Aspect of divinity, and His cooperation has been made possible through Christ's Own attainment along the line of the highest, spiritual will. He works under the great natural Law of Synthesis, producing at-one-ment, unification and fusion. His function (in unison with the energy of Christ) is to generate spiritual will in humanity, the will-to-good; His potency works in three fields of activity at this time:

a. Within the spiritual Hierarchy itself, revealing the nature of the divine will-to-good which the Kingdom of God must express, and the nature also of divine Purpose.
b. Within the Assembly of the United Nations, though not within the Security Council; He is there generating a slowly growing will-to-unity.
c. Within the masses of men everywhere, fostering the urge to a general betterment.

His activity is necessarily a mass activity, for He can only channel His energies through the mass consciousness or through a group conscious entity, such as the Hierarchy, the United Nations or Humanity. The focal point of His effort and the Agent through which distribution of His energy can be made is the New Group of World Servers;

this group is uniquely related to this Avatar of Synthesis. The bringing together of all the agents of goodwill (who are responsive to the energy of the divine will-to-good) constitutes the major objective of the New Group of World Servers and always has been. Their work can now be constructively and creatively intensified through the association of the Avatar of Synthesis with the Christ. Their task is to usher in the New Age; in that New Age, the five Kingdoms in Nature will begin to function as one creative whole. Their work falls into the following parts, functions or activities:

a. The production of a human synthesis or unity which will lead to an universal recognition of the *one humanity*, brought about through right human relations.
b. The establishing of right relations with the subhuman kingdoms in nature, leading to the universal recognition that there is *One World*.
c. The anchoring of the Kingdom of God, the spiritual Hierarchy of our planet, in open expression on Earth, thus leading to the universal recognition that the *sons of men are one*.

These objectives the Avatar of Synthesis will foster and aid and for this purpose He has associated Himself with the Christ, working through the Hierarchy, under instruction from the "centre where the will of God is known." These three related events and distributing points of energy have all come into activity during the point of tension in which Christ and the Hierarchy are at this time held. They all serve to re-direct and focus energy in relation to humanity, for all are the result of the decision made by Christ after His point of crisis, and are all connected with the hierarchical preparation for Christ's reappearance.

II. *Christ as the Forerunner of the Aquarian Age*

People are very apt to overlook the fact that though Christ recognised His function as Teacher and spiritual Leader of humanity during the age which is so rapidly drawing to a close, He also recognised the work which He would do when that age came to an end and the new astronomical cycle came into existence.

The average Christian is singularly unaware of the times and cycles through which our planet passes, under influence of solar progression. The at present dubious science of astrology has sidetracked the legitimate interest of humanity in the astronomical teaching and its spiritual interpretation of the passage of the Sun through the signs of the zodiac. Yet, in *The New Testament,* that recognition is clearly revealed and colours the presentation of the entire Gospel story. It is found also in *The Old Testament.* What was the sin of the Children of Israel in the desert but a reversion to the old Mithraic worship which distinguished the time when the sun was "in the sign of Taurus, the Bull," as it is technically called. They fell down and worshipped the golden calf and forgot the new teaching of the age of Aries, the Ram, into which they were entering, the teaching of the Scapegoat which colours Jewish history.

The fact that Christ was the Teacher of the new period into which the Sun was entering, the period of Pisces, is forgotten, but is clearly evidenced in the fish symbology which runs consistently through all four Gospels; the symbol of the Fish is the astrological symbol for the sign Pisces, and has been for untold ages. But Christ also looked ahead to the work He would have to do in the Aquarian Age, in the next sign into which the sun would enter. Prior to His "disappearance," He referred to the symbol of the Aquarian Age and to the task He would then perform. With His twelve disciples, He enacted a dramatic episode which epitomises the work which He would later undertake when the two thousand years of the Piscean era would have passed away. He told His disciples to go into the city and that there they would meet a man, carrying a pitcher of water, that they should follow him to the upper room and there make ready the communion feast in which He and they would share. (Luke XXII.10.) This they did and the Last Supper took place. The ancient symbol for the sign Aquarius (into which our Sun is now entering) is that of the Water-carrier, the man with a pitcher of water. This passing of the Sun into the sign Aquarius is an astronomical fact, as any one can ascertain by writing to any observatory; it is not an astrological prognostication. The great spiritual achievement and evolutionary event of that age will be the communion and human relationships established among all peoples, enabling men everywhere to sit down together in the Presence of the Christ and *share* the bread and wine (symbols of nourishment). Preparations for that shared feast (symbolically speaking) are on their way, and those preparations are being made by the masses of men themselves, as they fight and struggle and legislate for the economic sustenance of their nations, and as the theme of food occupies the attention of legislators everywhere. This sharing, beginning on the physical plane, will prove equally true of all human relations and this will be the great gift of the Aquarian Age to humanity. This the church has ignored and yet their ecclesiastics cannot explain away the fact that the Jews demonstrated

THE WORK OF THE CHRIST 81

their liking for the Taurian worship of the Bull in the golden calf, that the Jewish dispensation used the symbol of the scapegoat or ram in the age of Aries, the Ram, and that the Christian emphasises the fish in the Piscean era, the Christian era.

Christ came to bring to an end the Jewish dispensation which should have climaxed and passed away as a religion with the movement of the sun out of Aries into Pisces. He, therefore, presented Himself to them as their Messiah, manifesting through the Jewish race. In the rejection of the Christ as the Messiah, the Jewish race has remained symbolically and practically in the sign Aries, the Scapegoat; they have to pass—again speaking symbolically—into the sign, Pisces, the Fishes, and recognise their Messiah when He comes again in the sign Aquarius. Otherwise, they will repeat their ancient sin of non-response to the evolutionary process. They rejected that which was new and spiritual in the desert; they did it again in Palestine two thousand years ago; will they do it again, as opportunity is offered to them? The difficulty with the Jew is that he remains satisfied with the religion of nearly five thousand years ago and shows as yet little desire to change.

The coming in of the Aquarian Age, Christ foresaw and reduced to pictorial form for us, thus preserving for us—down the centuries—a prophetic episode, the interpretation of which is possible of demonstration only in our time and age. Astronomically, we are not yet functioning fully within the influence of Aquarius; we are only just emerging from the Piscean influence, and the full impact of the energies which Aquarius will set loose has not yet been felt. Nevertheless, each year carries us closer to the centre of power, the major effect of which will be to induce recognition of man's essential unity, of the processes of sharing and of cooperation and of the emergence of that new world religion whose keynote will be universality and initiation. If the word "initiation" signifies the processes of "entering into," then it is indeed true today that humanity is undergoing a true initiation as it enters into the new age of Aquarius; it will then be subjected to those energies and forces which will break down the barriers of separation, and which will blend and fuse the consciousness of all men into that unity which is distinctive of the Christ consciousness.

In June, 1945, at the time of the full moon (so significant a day in the spiritual experience of the Christ), He definitely and consciously took over His duties and responsibilities as the Teacher and Leader during the Aquarian solar cycle. He is the first of the great world Teachers to cover two zodiacal cycles—the Piscean and the Aquarian. This is a statement easily made and written down, but again it involves the three modes or techniques of appearance to which I have already referred. His outpouring love and spiritual vitality (augmented by the energies of the Spirit of Peace, the Avatar of Synthesis and the Buddha) were refocussed and channelled into a great stream, pulled through into expression (if I may word it so inadequately) by the words of the Invocation, "Let love stream forth into the hearts of men. . . . Let Light and Love and Power restore the Plan on Earth."

In those three words—light, love and power—the energies of His three Associates (the great Triangle of Force which stands in power behind Him) are described: the energy of the Buddha: Light, for the light ever comes from the East; the energy of the Spirit of Peace: Love, establishing right human relations; the energy of the Avatar of Synthesis: Power, implementing both light and love. At the centre of this Triangle the Christ took His

THE WORK OF THE CHRIST

stand; from that point His Aquarian work began, and it will continue for two thousand five hundred years. Thus He inaugurated the new era and, upon the inner spiritual planes, the new world religion began to take form. The word "religion" concerns relationship, and the era of right human relations and of a right relation to the Kingdom of God began. Such a statement as this is easily made but its implications are far-reaching and stupendous.

At that time also, the Christ assumed two new functions: one is connected with the second mode of His physical appearance and the other with the mode of over-shadowing. Over the masses, light, love and power are being poured forth and the growth of the Christ-consciousness is, therefore, being constantly stimulated. By His physical Presence, He will become the *"Dispenser of the Water of Life"*; through the over-shadowing of those sensitive to His impression and of His focussed Mind, He becomes what is technically known as the *"Nourisher of the little ones."*

As Dispenser of the Water of Life and as Nourisher of the Little Ones, He enters upon His duties in the Aquarian Age, whilst as the centre of the Triangle above mentioned, He influences, enlightens, and produces right relations in the masses of men. In the coming era, He will, therefore, be known as

1. The Point within the Triangle.
2. The Dispenser of the Water of Life.
3. The Nourisher of the Little Ones.

These are descriptive of His threefold duties to mankind, and of the work which will be distinctive of His world service, throughout the Aquarian Age.

Let us look at these phases of His work and try to understand the significance of the responsibility which He has undertaken. Some understanding is necessary if the New Group of World Servers and the working disciples in the world are to prepare mankind adequately for His appearing. Much can be done if men will apply themselves to comprehension and to the needed subsequent activity.

First, as the *Point within the Triangle,* Christ becomes the awakener of the hearts of men, and the one who institutes right human relations by being simply what He is and by standing unmoved where He is. This He accomplishes by transmitting the energies from the three points of the surrounding Triangle to humanity. This blended, impersonal energy, triple in nature, will be spread abroad universally, producing evolutionary growth, attracting people and nations magnetically to each other and automatically causing the unfoldment of the sense of synthesis, of provable unity and of a desirable fusion. Just as, during the Piscean Age, there was unfolded in humanity a mass responsiveness to knowledge and to the principle of intelligence, so in the Aquarian Age, a mass response to right relations will equally be evoked, and goodwill (as its expression) will be distinctive of the mass consciousness. It may be difficult to realise and appreciate this possibility but it was equally difficult for the mass of men in the first centuries of the Christian or Piscean era to realise the future growth of the educational systems of the world and the spread of that knowledge which is distinctive of our present civilisation and culture. Past attainment is ever the guarantee of future possibility.

As *Dispenser of the Water of Life,* His work is most mysterious and not at all easy to comprehend. In His public work, two thousand years ago, He said: "I am come

THE WORK OF THE CHRIST

that they may have life and that they may have it more abundantly." (John X.10.) The Life Aspect—from the angle of the vision of Christ—expresses itself in three ways:

1. *As physical life,* nourishing the cells of the body. This life is found within each atom of substance as the central point of living light.
2. *As livingness,* seen as love and light within the heart. When this livingness is present and expressing itself, the human atom becomes a part of the spiritual Hierarchy.
3. *As Life more abundantly.* This life can be known as light, love and power within and above the head of the disciple of the Christ. This abundant life enables him to cooperate, not only with humanity and with the spiritual Hierarchy, but also with Shamballa itself—the centre of life in its purest essence.

If we say that *life is the livingness which enables*, the words are relatively meaningless, are they not? If, however, the livingness is referred to the physical plane life, to the spiritual life of the disciple and to the living purpose of God, then some faint concept may come of the wonder of the work undertaken by the Christ in the past, and foreseen by Him as His future responsibility. Christ can draw upon the energies which are defined by the phrase "life more abundantly," because they will set loose (in the Aquarian Age) in a new and dynamic manner the new energies needed in order to bring about restoration and resurrection. This new energy is the "implementing force of universality"; it concerns the future. This inflow of Aquarian energy is one of the factors which will enable the Christ to complete His task as world Saviour and world Teacher. It was to the definite performance of His duties as Distributor, Nourisher and Dispenser that He pledged Himself in June, 1945, and entered upon His responsibilities as the Forerunner and the Teacher of the Aquarian Age.

As *Nourisher of the Little Ones,* we are dealing with an aspect of Christ's work which involves the stimulation of the consciousnesses of His disciples as they prepare to undergo initiation or to enter into deeper phases of spiritual awareness. The result of His work in the Triangle with the masses of men will be the presentation of the first initiation—the Birth of the Christ in the cave of the Heart—as the basic ceremony in the new world religion. By means of this ceremony, the masses of men in all lands will be enabled to register consciously the "birth of the Christ" in the heart, and the "being born again" to which He Himself referred (John III.3) when here on Earth before. *This new birth is what esotericists mean when they speak of the first initiation.* It will not, in the future, be the experience of the occasional disciple but the general experience of countless thousands towards the close of the Aquarian Age. The purifying waters of the Baptism Initiation (the second initiation) will submerge hundreds of aspirants in many lands, and these two initiations (which are preparatory to true service, and the third initiation of the Transfiguration) will set the seal on Christ's mission as the Agent of the great spiritual Triangle which He represents.

The major work of Christ, however, as far as the disciples and the definitely spiritually-minded people of the world are concerned, plus the hundreds of thousands of advanced humanity, is so to "nourish" their spiritual consciousness and life that they will be enabled to take the third and fourth initiations—those of the Transfiguration and the Renunciation (or Crucifixion).

As esotericists know, the term "little ones" refers to those disciples who are "babes in Christ" (as *The New Testament* terms it) and who have taken the first two initiations of the Birth and the Baptism. They are aware of the spiritual aspiration which is indicative of the Christ life in their hearts, and they have subjected themselves to the processes of purification which culminate in the baptismal waters. Christ must prepare these aspirants for the higher initiations and so nourish and aid them that they can stand before the One Initiator and become pillars in the Temple of God (i.e., agents of the spiritual Hierarchy and, therefore, active, working disciples).

When He was in Palestine, centuries ago, He said, "No man cometh unto the Father but by me." (John XIV.6.) This was a foretelling of the work which He would be called upon to do in the Aquarian era. In the first two initiations, aspirants (trained by senior disciples) find their way to Christ, Who administers the first two initiations; but—in these words—He is referring to still higher states of unfoldment. Through these initiations, administered by the Christ, the disciple becomes an agent of the love of God; the higher initiations enable him, however, to become, stage by stage, an agent of the will of God. The first group knows and understands the second stanza of the Invocation, "From the point of love within the heart of God, let love stream forth into the hearts of men"; the group which (in the Aquarian Age) the Christ Himself will "nourish" and prepare will know the meaning of the third stanza, "From the centre where the will of God is known, let purpose guide the little wills of men."

The work of Christ, during the Piscean Age, was to relate humanity to the Hierarchy of the planet; in the Aquarian Age, His work will be to relate this rapidly growing group to that higher centre where the Father is contacted, where recognition of sonship is accorded and where the divine purpose can be known. Through the coming work of Christ, the three divine aspects, recognised by all the world religions (including the Christian religion)—Intelligence or the Universal Mind, Love and Will—will be consciously developed in mankind; humanity, the spiritual Hierarchy and the "centre where the will of God is known" will be brought into a more open and general relationship.

The mystical approach to the Kingdom of God will gradually die out as the race achieves increasing intelligence and a more scientific approach will be favoured; the rules for admission into that Kingdom will become objective; the laws governing the highest centre of the divine will will also be revealed to those who are members of the Kingdom of God and all this will come about under the supervision of the Christ *after* His reappearance among men. The keynote of His mission then will be to evoke from humanity a response to spiritual influence and an unfoldment (on a large scale) of intuitive perception—a faculty which is, at present, rare indeed. When He came before, He evoked from humanity a gradual response to truth and mental understanding. That is why, at the end of the cycle which He inaugurated two thousand years ago, we have formulated doctrines and a widespread mental or intellectual development.

III. Christ as the Releaser of Energy

During the first three months of the period of crisis through which Christ and the Hierarchy passed and which

THE WORK OF THE CHRIST

was ended by His announced decision, certain great Energies, or fundamental streams of force were made available to Christ and His disciples. Today, the fact that energy is *the basic substance* in the universe, that all forms of life are energy forms, living within greater energy forms, and that all such forms—great or small—use energy and act as distributors of energy is a well-known and generally accepted fact by thinking and intelligent people. Speech, the written word, and motivated activity are all expressions of energy, lead to the spread of energy and to activities which are all expressions of energy and the cause of energy distribution. Governments, churches, organisations and groups are all energy distributors, and also storehouses of energy. Humanity itself is a great centre of energy, affecting all the subhuman kingdoms, and forming likewise within itself a great system of interrelated energies. The same thing is true of the individual who, by his acts and words, employs energy, produces effects which are energy effects and acts as a distributor of energy. Where the undeveloped individual is concerned, he realises none of this and the energy which he manipulates is of relatively small importance. As evolution proceeds, and individual men and women achieve power and expression, their use of energy *is* frequently of major importance; they become dynamic centres of energy distribution and their words (spoken or written), plus their activities, produce wide effects and momentous results. The Hierarchy is a great energy centre and, through the Christ, its energy reaches humanity; this is the significance of His words "I am come that they might have life." Life and energy are synonymous terms.

During the war (1914-1945), the Christ and the Hierarchy looked on at a dying world; men and forms were dying on every hand; old ideals, organisations and groups were passing away and the spectre of death stalked on every hand. Destruction characterised the phenomenal world, as well as the subtler worlds of feeling and of thought; life was withdrawn and death resulted. The problem of Christ and His disciples was to see that the old and the undesirable were not revivified. Their task was not the resuscitation of the dead and the useless; the directed inflow of life, carrying the capacity to build anew and the energy which could produce a new world and a new civilisation—there lay Their opportunity and Their responsibility.

The reactionary forces of the world—political and religious—desired the resurrection of the old and dead forms; they threw their weight and their influence (which is only another name for energy) against all that was new. This, they are still doing. The progressive forces fight only for that which is new, and seek not the preservation of any of the old forms, even if they could serve a useful purpose. Their energetic denial of all that is of the past, and the destroying energy which they direct against anything which is of the old regime are likewise handicapping the efforts of the Hierarchy. In these progressive forces, hope does indeed lie, but they sadly lack skill in action and have too great a love for destruction. The New Group of World Servers holds steadily to the "Noble Middle Way" (as the Buddha called it) and seeks the decent burial of old forms, the implementation of that which is new and the restoration of that which has, in the past, proved useful and good and which could form the living germ of the new creation.

At the time of the Full Moon of April 1945, during the Easter season of that year and covering approximately a period of five weeks, the Forces of Restoration began their work, emerging first upon the subtler planes

THE WORK OF THE CHRIST

of human experience. This type of energy is peculiarly creative in nature and carries the "life which produces the birth of forms." It poured into the Hierarchy, via certain of the Masters and Their groups of disciples, and was immediately transmitted by Them to humanity as a whole. This energy is a mass energy and is related to the stimulation of the mass intelligence; it is not the energy which we have earlier considered when dealing with the Christ consciousness in man. This is the energy which makes men think, plan and take action; it produces neither bad nor good results but simply brings about the awakening of men's minds so that they take intelligent action. That action is necessarily dependent upon the type of mind of the man who responds to the forces of restoration, conditioned by his point in evolution, his racial and national background, his tradition and his religious and civilised reactions. These forces are active now in every land, frequently producing increased initial difficulties but leading eventually to a definite reorganisation of the national or planetary life. Their effects will be primarily physical; they will bring about a new world in which the evidences of war will have disappeared, the physical health of men and animals will be bettered, and cities and villages will be rebuilt. Their objective is the production of the new Earth and all the outer evidences of an inflowing new life.

Following this inflow, at the time of the Full Moon of the Buddha in May 1945, the forces of enlightenment became active, and light began to stream into the minds of men. These are, in reality, the energies which initiate the new world education. Those first to be affected by them are the great educational movements, the forums of the people in all lands and the values which are now unfolding through the radio and the moving picture industry; others deeply affected are the press, the publishers of world literature, speakers, writers, radio commentators, newspaper men and social workers. These effects may not yet be apparent for little time has as yet elapsed, but all these movements and people are the recipients today of the energies of enlightenment *if* they are prompt to recognise new emerging ideas; they are the custodians of this energy and its distributing agents, channelling it and directing it so that the masses of the people everywhere come under its influence. Progressive and liberal churchmen in all the world religions are also responsive to this energy, but their usefulness is greatly handicapped, owing to the reactionary nature of the setting or field in which they have to work; they are confronted with a well-nigh impossible task.

These energies of enlightenment reach humanity, via the New Group of World Servers who are very susceptible to their impact, and who are in a position to distribute them, because they are to be found working in all the fields of activity mentioned above.

The forces of restoration are related to and emanate from the Mind of God and are connected with the intelligent principle in the divine nature; the intellect is that divine aspect which distinguishes man from all other forms in nature. The forces of enlightenment come from the Heart of God and are related to divine understanding and can, therefore, reach and strengthen all those who love and serve their fellowmen. This energy is related to the second aspect or principle of divinity, love-wisdom, of which the Buddha and the Christ are the two outstanding divine expressions. It is mainly through Them and Their disciples, or the Masters on the same line of divine expression, that these energies reach humanity, channeled by the New Group of World Servers.

THE WORK OF THE CHRIST

The Christ and the Buddha combined the Way of the Mind and the Way of the Heart in Their perfection, and towered above their fellowmen from the heights of Their achievement. They swayed hemispheres and centuries, whereas lesser sons of God sway countries and shorter periods of time. They still have some consummating work to carry through, though the indicated work lies not so much with the forms which embody Their enunciated divine principles—light and love—as with the souls who have evolved through the application of these principles.

In June 1945, Christ set in motion the forces of reconstruction which are related to the Will aspect of divinity and which remain as yet the least powerful of the three streams of energy, released during the three Full Moon Festivals in 1945. These forces of reconstruction are effective mainly in relation to those entities which we call *nations*. The Hierarchy is at this time attempting to channel them into the Assembly of the United Nations; the use made of these impersonal energies is dependent upon the quality and the nature of the recipient nation, on its measure of true enlightenment and on its point in evolution. *Nations are the expression today of the massed self-centredness of a people and of their instinct to self-preservation.* These energies can, therefore, increase that aspect of their lives. They can, however, and in spite of this, increase the potency of the objective which the United Nations (at present) *theoretically* hold before the eyes of men everywhere. The main object of the Hierarchy is so to distribute these constructive, synthesising energies that the theory of unity may slowly be turned into practice, and the word "United" may come to have a true significance and meaning. It is with this type of energy that the Avatar of Synthesis is peculiarly allied. He will convey to humanity, with the aid of the Christ, something for which we have as yet no name. It is neither love nor will, as we understand them. Only a phrase of several words will bring to us something of the meaning. This phrase is "the principle of directed Purpose." This principle involves three things:

1. Understanding—intuitive and spiritually instinctual, but intelligently interpreted—of the Plan, as it can be worked out in the immediate future by the Christ and His disciples.
2. Focussed intention, based upon the above and emphasising an aspect of the will, hitherto undeveloped in man.
3. Capacity to direct energy (through understanding and intent) towards a recognised and desired end, overcoming all obstacles and destroying all that stands in its way. This is not the destruction of forms by force such as we have seen imposed upon the world, but a destruction brought about by the greatly strengthened life within the form.

The significance of these divine principles will make little sense to us today; we are dealing with major mysteries. A mystery remains a mystery only when ignorance or unbelief exist. There is no mystery where there is knowledge and faith. All we know at this time is that the Christ will fuse and blend within Himself three principles of divinity; when He appears "the light that always has been will be seen; the love that never ceases will be realised, and the radiance, deep concealed, will break forth into Being." We shall then have a new world—one which will express the light, the love and the knowledge of God in a crescendo of revelation.

THE WORK OF THE CHRIST 95

The beauty of this synthesis which Christ will manifest, and the wonder of the presented opportunity, must surely be apparent to all of us. Great Forces, under potent spiritual Leadership, are standing ready to precipitate themselves into this world of chaos, of confusion, of aspiration, of hope and of bewilderment. These groups of energies are ready for focussing and distribution by the Hierarchy and that Hierarchy, under its Great Leader, the Christ, is closer to mankind than ever before in human history. The New Group of World Servers are also standing attentive to direction in every country in the world, united in their idealism, in their humanitarian objectives, in their sensitivity to spiritual impression, in their united, subjective purpose, in their love of their fellowmen and in their dedication to selfless service. The men and women of goodwill are also to be found everywhere, ready to be guided into constructive activity and to be the agents, gradually trained and educated, for the establishing of that which has never yet before truly existed—*right human relations*.

Thus from the highest spiritual Being upon our planet, through the graded spiritual groups of enlightened and perfected men who work upon the inner side of life, on into the outer world of daily living where thinking, loving men and women serve, the tide of the new life sweeps. The Plan is ready for immediate application and intelligent implementing; the workers are there and the power to work *is* adequate to the need. Above all else, the *Hierarchy stands* and the *Christ stands* ready to issue forth and demonstrate reality.

IV. *Christ, as the Unifier of East and West*

This is a hard saying for the orthodox and narrow Christian churchman to accept; it means primarily that

Christ will work in the closest cooperation with the Buddha until this fusion and reconstruction have truly taken place. The Buddha is closely allied with the Christ in this process of His reappearing, though He will not be involved or active during the entire period of Christ's coming, active work on earth. As you know, He, too, has not relinquished His contact and relationship with humanity, though He relinquished His physical body centuries ago. He did this in order to accomplish certain assigned work which had in it (besides many things unknown to humanity) activities connected with the work of the Christ, with the immediacy of His coming and with certain plans for the coming civilisation of the Aquarian Age. As many millions in the world know, each year (at the time of the Wesak Festival at the May Full Moon) He communicates with humanity, via the Christ and the assembled, attentive Hierarchy. He acts in this way as an agent bringing about relationship between the "centre where the will of God is known" and the "centre which we call the race of men." These two descriptive phrases are used advisedly because all the work now being done by these two great Sons of God is concerned with the distribution of energy—the energy of light and the energy of love. It is through the Triangle, earlier mentioned, that the energy of will eventually will be distributed and one of these divine distributors is the Buddha.

Actually the work of the Buddha for humanity is nearly over, and His long alliance with the race of men has nearly come to an end. The moment that the appearance of the Christ is an accomplished fact, and the rule of right human relations is beginning definitely to condition human living, then the Buddha will pass to the work which awaits Him. One of the senior disciples of the Christ, ranking next to the Christ in hierarchical status,

THE WORK OF THE CHRIST

will take His place and carry on the work, connected with mankind.

By the time this particular Master takes over His task, the intelligent principle or knowledge, which is the outstanding characteristic of humanity, will have been to a large extent transmuted into wisdom by the world intelligentsia, though not as yet by the masses of men. Wisdom is the predominant characteristic of the Buddha and the momentum of this wisdom energy will eventually be so strong that it will need no further distribution or control by the Buddha. He can then re-orient Himself to higher spheres of activity where His true work lies, and begin to work with an aspect of wisdom of which we know nothing but of which both knowledge and wisdom have been expressing themselves through the Christ and the Buddha; later, through the cooperation of the Avatar of Synthesis, Christ will be able to blend within Himself both of these major divine energies, and thus be a pure expression of love and wisdom, of right relationship and intuitive understanding.

In order to make this possible and thus release His spiritual Brother from the arduous task of relating humanity to the "centre where the will of God is known" (Shamballa), Christ is subjecting Himself at this time to an unique process of training. Of this training, His thirty years of work in the carpenter's shop in Palestine has ever been the hitherto unrecognised symbol. The word "carpenter" is significant of building, of construction, and means (in its derivation) someone who is an artificer in timber or a builder of wooden houses. This is the true meaning of the Biblical story of Christ's being crucified upon the cross of wood or the tree. It is related in reality to the decision made by Christ in the Garden of Gethsemane to take over the building or reconstruction work in Aquarius, and thus complete the task which He attempted to do in the Piscean Age. He and His disciples and the New Group of World Servers are the pledged *builders* of the new civilisation, the new "house of humanity." The preparatory work He is now doing will fit Him to demonstrate in wisdom (and not only through love) the nature of the hierarchical Plans, wise constructive measures, wise choice of builders and correct methods of construction.

It is apparent, therefore, that this greatest of the Sons of God, the Christ, Representative of humanity and of the second divine aspect, will demonstrate within Himself, during the Aquarian Age and after His reappearance, certain major fused and blended dualities. It would profit us to study them and know which they are:

1. The fusion of the second divine aspect of Love and the first divine aspect of Will—the Will-to-good.
2. The fusion of love and wisdom, enabling Him to be the Builder of the new age and civilisation.
3. The fusion of Piscean energy, generated during the past two thousand years of Christ's spiritual activity and the Aquarian energies to be generated and active on Earth during the next two thousand years, or two thousand five hundred.

It is for this process of fusion and all that it entails that He now subjects Himself to training. When this is completed, He can become in a sense hitherto unknown to Him the focal point and the transmitting Agent for all these five divine energies:

1. The energy of Love.
2. The energy of Will.

3. The energy of Wisdom.
4. Piscean energy, generated during the Christian era.
5. Aquarian energy, already generating upon the inner planes of thought and feeling, and to be generated during the centuries ahead of us.

The lines which His training follows are known only to Christ, to the Buddha and to the Avatar of Synthesis. All esoteric or spiritual training has to be self-applied; this is as true of the Christ as it is of the humblest aspirant. Into the processes of Christ's thinking, reactions and planning, it is not possible for us to enter.

In Palestine, His appearance was mainly prophetic and His work primarily that of laying the foundation for the activities which will follow His reappearance, plus the sowing of the seed, the harvest of which He will garner in the new age. The tragedy of His appearance two thousand years ago has coloured the presentation of truth by the theologians and made them posit an unhappy story, producing a miserable and unhappy world. This tragedy was based on:

1. His discovery that humanity was not ready for that which He came to give and that for centuries much experience, teaching, trial and testing would be needed before His real work could begin.
2. His recognition that He Himself needed a deeper relation with that centre which He always referred to as "the Father's House"; it was this realisation which led to His comment that His disciples could and would do "greater things" than He had done and that He had to go to His Father.
3. His arriving at the conclusion that He must have more trained and dedicated workers and agents

than at that time was possible, or has proved possible since. Hence the gathering out and the training of the New Group of World Servers. When there are enough of these servers and enlightened workers, He will come and nothing can arrest His approach.

4. He discovered also that men were not then desperate enough to "take the Kingdom of Heaven by violence"; it is only in desperation and when completely at the end of his tether that the disciple finds his way into that Kingdom and is ready to relinquish the old ways. What is true of the individual must also be true, on a larger scale, of humanity.

It is to the whole world that Christ comes and not just to the Christian world. He comes to the East and to the West, and has foreseen this "time of the end," with its planetary catastrophes, phenomenal disasters, despair and invocation—arising from both the East and West. He knew that in the time of final crisis and tension, humanity itself would force His emergence. *The New Testament* story is true and correct; it is only the man-made interpretations which have misled humanity.

In the East there is an ancient legend which has an application today and which holds the clue to the relation of the Christ and of the Buddha; it concerns a service which, the legend says, the Buddha will render Christ. In symbolic form, the legend runs that when the Buddha reached enlightenment, and experience on Earth could teach Him no more, He looked ahead to the time when His Brother, the Christ, would be active in the Great Service—as it is called. In order, therefore, to aid the Christ, He left behind Him (for His use) what are mysteriously called "His vestures." He bequeathed and left

THE WORK OF THE CHRIST

in some safe place the sumtotal of His emotional-intuitive nature, called by some the astral body and the sum total of His knowledge and His thought, called His mind or mental body. These, the legend says, will be assumed by the Coming One and prove of service, supplementing Christ's Own emotional and mental equipment and providing Him with what He needs as the Teacher of the East as well as of the West. He can then with strength and success contemplate His future work and choose His workers. There is something of this same idea latent in the injunction given in *The New Testament,* "Let this mind be in you which was also in Christ." (Phil. II:5.)

Thus the Christ, with the fused energies of love and wisdom, with the aid of the Avatar of Synthesis and of the Buddha and under the influence of the Spirit of Peace and of Equilibrium, can implement and direct the energies which will produce the coming new civilisation. He will see, demonstrating before His eyes the true resurrection—the emergence of mankind from the imprisoning cave of materialism. Thus He will "see of the travail of His soul and shall be satisfied." (Is. LIII:11.)

CHAPTER FIVE

THE TEACHINGS OF THE CHRIST

The Establishing of Right Human Relations
The Law of Rebirth
Revelation of the Mystery of Initiation
The Dispelling of Glamour

IT MIGHT be useful to make a few opening remarks upon the general subject of the teaching given (down the ages) by the Sons of God Who have come forth in the hour of humanity's need, in order to present to the consciousness of the men of Their time certain required ideas and concepts of truth. When They come, Their aim is to meet the immediate need in such a fashion that the ideas presented may become ideals to which eventually the life of mankind would later conform and bring about a better civilisation. There has been a great continuity of such teaching down the ages.

There is not the time to write or the time to read a complete analysis or statement as to the progressive revelation of ideas which great and illumined minds, authorised by the spiritual Hierarchy of the planet, have brought to humanity. All the cyclic Teachers (to differentiate Them from the many lesser Teachers) have mastered life for Themselves in the three worlds of human evolution—physical, emotional and mental—have achieved control of the physical level of consciousness, of Their emotional-feeling nature, and have attained mental understanding and finally enlightenment.

The problem of the Hierarchy has been (and still is) how much exact truth humanity can comprehend, and to

THE TEACHINGS OF THE CHRIST

what extent absolute truth can be presented to their awakening minds; They have to decide which aspect of universal truth will enable man to emerge out of his difficulties and thus move forward on the Path of Return to God; They have to know, therefore, at what point on the ladder of evolution humanity stands at any given period. This in itself presents a field of research to Them.

The method hitherto followed has been to decide what is the major factor lacking in man's perception of reality (at any given time), and what recognised divine truth has in it the seeds of a living activity for a humanity in a particular condition, necessitating a certain type of help. They have also to determine how that help can best be presented, so that its results will be lasting, cultural and effective. Hitherto, the presented concepts have been formulated by the world Teachers of the period, and presented to a picked and chosen few whose task it has been to take the newly presented idea and promulgate it among those men who are enlightened enough to accept it, to spread it, to live it and to make it popular. This they have done for ages with more or less success.

It is also not possible here to give the relatively few truths which guided the development of humanity in old Atlantis; these, however, form the firm foundation of all later teaching. We can study (as a background to our consideration of the teachings which Christ will give *after* His reappearance) several of the minor concepts which today underlie the teaching of all the world religions, and which modern religious teachers should be presenting to the public mind.

The first such Teacher is of such ancient date that it is not possible to say when He truly lived; even His name is a modernised one, given to ·an ancient hero-teacher. His name is *Hercules*. He presented to the world, through the form of a pictorial and world drama (symbolic in nature) the concept of a great objective, only to be reached as the result of struggle and difficulty. He pointed to a goal toward which men must make their way, no matter what the obstacles; these obstacles He portrayed in the Twelve Labours of Hercules which were dramas and not factual occurrences. He thus pictured for those who had eyes to see and hearts to understand the nature of the problem to be solved upon the Path of Return to God; He depicted the Prodigal Son's journey back to the Father's house, and the tests and trials which all disciples, aspirants and initiates have to face and which all Those Who today compose the spiritual Hierarchy have already faced. When this statement is considered, it must include also the Christ Who, we are told, "was in all points tempted like as we are" (Heb. IV:15), but also passed triumphantly the tests and trials.

At some also unknown date *Hermes* came and, so the records say, was the first to proclaim Himself as "the Light of the World." Later the great Teacher, *Vyasa,* appeared. He gave one simple and needed message that death is not the end. From His time, the thinking of humanity about the possible immortality of the soul can be seen to stem. Vaguely and instinctively, men had hoped and sensed that the discarding of the physical vehicle was not the final consummation to all human struggle, loving and aspiration; in those early days, feeling dominated and instinct led; thought was not found among the masses of men as it is today. In this period of culmination in which we now live, the work of the spiritualistic movement, in its many forms, is in reality the emergence of that stream of thought-energy and of the idea which Vyasa, thousands of years ago, implanted in the human consciousness. The effort of the intellectuals to prove the scientific possibility of immortality is part also of this great stream, carried onto intellectual levels, thus salvaging Vyasa's work from the mists and glamours and the psychic dishonesty with which it is now surrounded. The fact of immortality is today on the verge of scientific proof; the fact of the survival of some factor has already been proved, though what has been demonstrated as surviving is apparently not in itself intrinsically immortal. The factual nature of the soul, and the fact of soul survival and of its eternal livingness, go hand in hand and have not yet been scientifically proven; they are, however, known and recognised as truths today by such countless millions and by so many intellectuals that—unless mass hysteria and mass deception is posited—their existence is already correctly surmised.

Buddha is the next Teacher to Whom we should refer, though there were many between His time and that of Vyasa. During those centuries wherein history is relatively dim and faint in its outlines, the intelligence of men had been rapidly growing, and the enquiring perception of mankind came into increasingly active use. The asking of questions, to which there seem no apparent or easy answers, focussed itself in a group of thinkers in India and they represented thinking men in every land. They asked the ancient questions as to why there is sorrow and misery in every land and in every life; they asked what caused these things and what must be done to change these circumstances of life; they demanded to know what was the integrating principle in man, and what was the soul and was there a self. The Buddha came forth to give the answer and to lay the foundation for a more enlightened approach to life, giving the teaching which would open the door to the work of the Christ Who would, He knew, follow in His steps.

It is interesting to remember that when the Buddha came, approximately five hundred years before Christ (for the exact date of Christ's birth remains debatable), the first dim influences of the Piscean Age could be felt, impinging upon the powerful quality of the age of Aries, the Scapegoat or the Ram. It was the influence of this age—persisting throughout the Jewish dispensation—which led eventually to the distortion of the simple teaching of the Christ when He came. He was erroneously presented to the world as the living Scapegoat, bearing away the sins of the people, and thus originating the doctrine of the vicarious at-one-ment. It was St. Paul who was responsible for this emphasis. A parallelling instance of a similar distortion was also of Jewish origin and appeared in the early stages of the cycle of Aries, the Ram. We are told that the Children of Israel fell down and worshipped the golden calf, the symbol of Taurus, the Bull; this was the preceding astronomical cycle. These are astronomical cycles and not a presented astrology. In the early stages of Aries, the teaching reverted to that of Taurus and in the early stages of Pisces, it reverted to that of Aries and thus set the seal of retrogression upon the teaching which now controls so many orthodox Christians.

Buddha answered the questions posited in His time by giving out the *Four Noble Truths,* which satisfactorily and eternally answer man's demand of *why*. These Truths can be summarised as follows: the Buddha taught that misery and suffering were of man's own making and that the focussing of human desire upon the undesirable, the ephemeral and the material was the cause of all despair, all hatred and competition, and the reason why

THE TEACHINGS OF THE CHRIST

man found himself living in the realm of death—the realm of physical living, which is the true death of the spirit. He made a unique contribution to the teaching given by Hercules and Vyasa, and added to the structure of truth which They had erected. Thus He prepared the way for Christ. Between the times of these two great Teachers, the Buddha and the Christ, lesser teachers appeared to amplify and add to the already given basic truths; of these Sankaracharya was one of the most important, giving, as He did, deep instruction upon the nature of the Self. Also the teacher in *The Bhagavad Gita,* Shri Krishna, must be noted, for many believe Him to be a previous incarnation of the Christ.

Thus the fundamental truths upon which relation to God (and, therefore, relation to our fellowmen) is founded are always given out by the Son of God, Who—in any particular world period—is the teaching Head of the spiritual Hierarchy.

In due time, *Christ* came and gave out to the world (mainly through His disciples) two major truths: the fact of the existence of the human soul and, secondly, the system of service (this phrase is used advisedly) as a mode of establishing right human relations—to God and to one's fellowmen. He told men that they were all the Sons of God in the same sense that He was; He told them in many symbolic ways who and what He was and assured them that they could do even greater things than He had done, because they were divine as He was. These greater things, humanity has already accomplished upon the physical plane and in its control of nature, as Christ knew men would, because He knew the workings of the Law of Evolution. He taught them that service was the key to the life of liberation, teaching them the technique of service through His own life as He went about doing good, healing the sick, as well as preaching and teaching the things of the Kingdom of God and feeding the hungry, both physically and spiritually. He made the life of every day a divine sphere of spiritual livingness, thus emphasising the teaching of the Buddha, through desiring nothing for the separated self. Thus the Christ taught, loved, and lived, carrying forward the great continuity of revelation and of hierarchical teaching; then He entered for us within the veil, leaving us an example that we should follow His steps (1 Pet. II:21)—follow Him in His belief in divinity, in His service and in ability to penetrate into that area of consciousness and that field of activity which we call the true Church of Christ, the spiritual (at present invisible) Hierarchy of our planet, the true Kingdom of God. The veil that hides that real church from us is now in process of disappearing and Christ is on the verge of reappearing.

In the light of the past, therefore, and of humanity's present need, which Christ and the Hierarchy must meet, what will be the teaching which He will this time give? Such is the question which His disciples are now asking. The probability is that His teaching will fall into four parts; we would do well to consider each of them and do our best to understand and prepare the human mind for the reception of what He has to give.

I. *The Establishing of Right Human Relations*

The phrase "right human relations" is one that is today being much discussed; it is being increasingly realised that it is a major human need, and the only hope of a peaceful and secure future. Wrong human relations have reached such a stage of difficulty that every phase of human life is in a state of chaotic turmoil; every aspect of daily living is involved—family life, communal living, business relations, religious and political contacts, governmental action and the habitual life of all peoples, including the entire field of international relations. Everywhere there is hate, competition, mal-adjustment, strife between parties, the vilest kind of muck raking and scandal making, deep distrust between men and nations, between capital and labour and among the many sects, churches and religions. The difference between a sect and a church is, after all, only one of degree and historical inception; it is one of interpretation, of fanatical adherence to some pet truth and always—exclusiveness, which is contrary to Christian teaching. Nowhere is there peace today or understanding; only a small minority in relation to the Earth's population are struggling for those conditions which will lead to peaceful and happy relationships.

The strength of this fighting minority, struggling for peace and right relations, consists in the fact that the work they are attempting to do is in line with divine intention and purpose. Into this chaos of conflicting, competitive and fighting interests, Christ plans to reappear. I would ask you to contemplate the very real horror of what He has to face, and the necessity for some measure of order to be brought about in the world, for certain basic principles to be enunciated and partially, at least, accepted, before He can usefully work amongst men. If He were to come immediately, His voice would not be heard, for the noise of men's quarrelling is too great; if He sought to attract human attention, even through the prophesied sound of the trumpet (Matt. XXIV:31), He would be classed simply as one who advertised himself; if He preached and taught, He would attract primarily those who think naturally in unison with His message, or the gullible and the credulous would flock to Him, as they do to all new teachers—no matter what they teach. The bulk of human beings are still too hungry, too devastated psychically, too bewildered and distressed, and too unsure of their future, their freedom and their security to be in any condition to listen to Him.

He will not come, we may be sure, as a conquering hero, as the interpretations of the theological teachers have led man to believe, for that would certainly fail to identify Him and He would be simply classed as another military figure; of them we have had a plethora; He will not come as the Messiah of the Jews to save the so-called Holy Land and the city of Jerusalem for the Jews, because He belongs to the whole world and no Jews nor any other people have special rights or unique privileges or may claim Him as their own; He will not come to convert the "heathen" world for, in the eyes of the Christ and of His true disciples, no such world exists and the so-called heathen have demonstrated historically less of the evil of vicious conflict than has the militant Christian world. The history of the Christian nations and of the Christian church has been one of an aggressive militancy —the last thing desired by the Christ when He sought to establish the church on earth.

When He came before He said (and the words have been sadly misread): "I come not to bring peace but a sword" (Matt. X:34). This will be true especially during the early days of His advent. The sword which He wields is the sword of the Spirit; it is that sword which produces cleavage between a true spirituality and an habitual materialism. The major effect of His appearance will surely be to demonstrate in every land the effects of *a spirit of inclusiveness*—an inclusiveness which will be channelled or expressed through Him. All who seek right human relations will be gathered automatically to Him,

THE TEACHINGS OF THE CHRIST

whether they are in one of the great world religions or not; all who see no true or basic difference between religion and religion or between man and man or nation and nation will rally around Him; those who embody the spirit of exclusiveness and separativeness will stand automatically and equally revealed and all men will know them for what they are. The cleaving sword of the spirit will—without wounding—bring revelation and indicate the first needed step towards human regeneration.

Standing as the focal point of the inner Triangle—of the Buddha, of the Spirit of Peace and of the Avatar of Synthesis—the consequent outpouring potency of the Christ will be so great that the distinction between love and hate, between aggression and freedom, and between greed and sharing will be made lucidly clear to the eyes and minds of all men and, therefore, the distinction between good and evil will be made equally clear. The invocative prayer, "From the point of love within the heart of God, let love stream forth into the hearts of men" will meet with fulfillment. Christ will let loose into the world of men the potency and the distinctive energy of intuitive love. The results of the distribution of this energy of love will be twofold:

1. Countless men and women in every land will form themselves into groups for the promotion of goodwill and for the production of right human relations. So great will be their numbers that from being a small and relatively unimportant minority, they will be the largest and the most influential force in the world. Through them, the New Group of World Servers will be able to work successfully.
2. This active energy of loving understanding will mobilise a tremendous reaction against the potency

of hate. To hate, to be separate, and to be exclusive will come to be regarded as the only sin, for it will be recognised that all the sins—as listed and now regarded as wrong—only stem from hate or from its product, the anti-social consciousness. Hate and its dependent consequences are the true sin against the Holy Ghost, about which commentators have so long debated, overlooking (in their silliness) the simplicity and the appropriateness of the true definition.

The power of the hierarchical spiritual impact, focussed through Christ and His working disciples, will be so great that the usefulness, the practicality and the naturalness of right human relations will become so evident that world affairs will rapidly be adjusted and the new era of goodwill and of peace on earth will be inaugurated. The new culture and the new civilisation will then be possible.

This is the picture of no optimistic, mystical and impossible event. It is not based upon wishful thinking or upon a blind hope. Already today, the disciples of the Christ are preaching the doctrine of right human relations; men and women of goodwill are endeavouring to show that only through goodwill can true peace be brought about in the arena of international life. In the presentation of true "livingness" which the Christ will demonstrate to the world of thinking men, there is necessarily no room for exclusiveness or for separativeness, because that "life more abundantly" (which He seeks to channel to us) is a free and flowing current, sweeping away obstructions and barriers, and establishing an unimpeded circulation of truth and life itself—the essential quality of both being *love*.

All the world religions have posited the fact that God is Love essentially and that God is life essentially as well as intelligence. That life carries within itself the essential quality of the will of God, as well as the love of God. Both are equally important because that will is qualified by love. Hitherto, men have known nothing of the factual nature of the quality of livingness, energised by love and will, except through a vague theoretical conception. The reappearance of Christ will establish the fact of this divine livingness; the work which He will accomplish—with the aid of His disciples—will demonstrate the love and the divine purpose which lie behind all phenomenal experience.

The establishing of right human relations is an aspect of the divine will for humanity and the next facet of the divine expression to manifest itself in human affairs—individual, communal, national, and international. Nothing has ever finally impeded this divine expression, except the *time* factor, and that time factor is *determined by humanity* and is an expression of divine freewill. The intended, divine expression can move rapidly or slowly into manifestation, according as man decides; hitherto, man has decided upon a slow—a very slow—manifestation. It is here that the freedom of the human will shows itself. Because divinity is immanent or present in all forms and, therefore, in all human beings, that will *must* eventually be fulfilled; because of the tremendously material intention (esoterically speaking) of all forms at present, that Will has hitherto been retarded in its expression; it has *not* been the will of man to establish right human relations. Hence the discipline of war, the torture of the forms, and the misery in human living today.

These factors are bringing about a great and general transformation; the indications of this are easily to be seen by spiritually minded people. Such people are constantly saying (as Christ did in the Garden of Gethsemane), "Let the will of God be done." (Matt. XXVI:39.) They say it ignorantly and often hopelessly; nevertheless, it indicates a general process of spiritual re-orientation, of submission and of acquiescence. Christ demonstrated this *submission* when He said, "I came not to do my own will but the will of Him Who sent me." (John VI:38.) He proved His *acquiescence* when He cried, "Father, not my will but Thine be done." Submission has in it the elements of conquest by circumstances and of a recognition which may not understand but which submits to that which is imposed. Acquiescence has in it the element of an understanding intelligence, and this marks a great step forward. Both admit the fact of a divine over-shadowing will in the life of mankind today; both are preparatory to a recognition of Christ's work in bringing about right human relations. At present, the submission of mankind to the divine will is a negative submission; the true submission is a positive attitude of spiritual expectancy, leading eventually to a positive acquiescence.

A spiritual expectancy is also to be seen; it is part of the work of the New Group of World Servers to intensify this. They have also to foster spiritual submission and intelligent acquiescence in the masses, who normally divide themselves into the two classes, expressing these two attitudes; these factors of submission, acquiescence and expectancy are latent in every man. It is these three divine potentialities which will enable men to respond to the message of the Christ and, therefore, the selfless sacrifice, the understanding compromise and the comprehension of the many and diverse points of view (neces-

THE TEACHINGS OF THE CHRIST 115

sary to the establishing of right human relations) will be far easier to bring about.

We would all find it helpful to reflect upon what are the factors recognised in submission and acquiescence. In establishing right human relations, relinquishment, renunciation, submission to existent facts, and obedient acquiescence to divine law are all involved. These are the things which Christ earlier demonstrated on Earth, and they are the things which He will help humanity to accept with enthusiasm and understanding. This will produce happiness. Happiness is a difficult lesson to learn; it is for mankind a totally new experience and Christ will have to teach men how to handle happiness correctly, to overcome the ancient habits of misery, and thus to know the meaning of true joy. Christ, however, is not coming simply to teach men the need for right human relations; He is coming to teach them how to establish it successfully themselves.

II. Christ Will Teach the Law of Rebirth

This Law is the major corollary of the Law of Evolution. It has never been grasped or properly understood in the West and, in the East, where it is acknowledged as a governing principle of life, it has not proved useful because it has been soporific in its effect, and a detriment to progress. The Eastern student regards it as giving him plenty of time; this has negated the driving effort to achieve a goal. The average Christian confuses the Law of Rebirth with what he calls "the transmigration of souls," and frequently believes that the Law of Rebirth signifies the passing of human beings into the bodies of animals or of lower forms of life. Such is by no means the case. As the life of God progresses onwards through form after form, that life in the subhuman kingdoms of nature proceeds progressively from mineral forms into vegetable forms, and from these vegetable forms into animal forms; from the animal form stage, the life of God passes into the human kingdom, and becomes subject to the Law of Rebirth and *not* the law of Transmigration. To those who know something of the Law of Rebirth or of Reincarnation, the mistake seems ridiculous.

The doctrine or theory of reincarnation strikes the orthodox Christian with horror; yet if one asks him the question which the disciples asked Christ about the blind man, "Master, did this man sin or his fathers that he was born blind?" (John IX:2), they refuse the implications; or they express amusement or dismay as the case may be. The presentation to the world of the thought by the average occult or theosophical exponent has been, on the whole, deplorable. It has been deplorable because it has been so unintelligently presented. The best that can be said is that they have familiarised the general public with the theory; had it, however, been more intelligently presented, it might have been more generally accepted in the West.

If the goal of right human relations will be taught universally by the Christ, the emphasis of His teaching *must* be laid upon the Law of Rebirth. This is inevitably so, because in the recognition of this law will be found the solution of all the problems of humanity, and the answer to much of human questioning.

This doctrine will be one of the keynotes of the new world religion, as well as the clarifying agent for a better understanding of world affairs. When Christ was here, in person, before, He emphasised the fact of the soul and the value of the individual. He told men that they could be saved by the life of the soul, and of the Christ within

THE TEACHINGS OF THE CHRIST 117

the human heart. He said also that "except a man be born again, he cannot see the Kingdom of God." (John III:3.) Only *souls* can function as citizens of that kingdom, and it was this privileged functioning that He held, for the first time, before humanity, thus giving men a vision of a divine possibility and an unalterable conclusion to experience. He told them to "Be ye, therefore, perfect, even as your Father which is in Heaven is perfect." (Matt. V:48.)

This time, He will teach men the method whereby this possibility can become accomplished fact—through the constant return of the incarnating soul to the school of life on Earth, there to undergo the perfecting process of which He was the outstanding example. That is the meaning and teaching of reincarnation. Dane Rudhyar, in his book *New Mansions for New Men,* page 123, gives a satisfying definition of this mysterious cosmic and human process. He says that "The individual structure of the new manifestation is necessarily conditioned by the unfulfillment of the past; by the remains, the failures of the past—preserved in the records of nature in the memory of universal substance." The whole story—yours and mine and that of everyone—is covered in those few words.

It should be remembered that practically all the occult groups and writings have foolishly laid the emphasis upon *past* incarnations and upon their recovery; this recovery is incapable of any reasonable checking—anyone can say and claim anything they like; the teaching has been laid upon imaginary rules, supposed to govern the time equation and the interval between lives, forgetting that time is a faculty of the brain-consciousness and that, divorced from the brain, time is non-existent; the emphasis has always been laid upon a fictional presentation of relationships. The teaching (hitherto given out on reincarnation) has done more harm than good. Only one factor remains of value: the existence of a Law of Rebirth is now discussed by many and accepted by thousands.

Beyond the fact that there is such a law, we know little and those who know from experience the factual nature of this return reject earnestly the foolish and improbable details, given out as fact by the theosophical and occult bodies. *The Law exists; of the details of its working we know as yet nothing.* Only a few things can be said with accuracy about it and these few warrant no contradiction:

1. The Law of Rebirth is a great natural law upon our planet.
2. It is a process, instituted and carried forward under the Law of Evolution.
3. It is closely related to and conditioned by the Law of Cause and Effect.
4. It is a process of progressive development, enabling men to move forward from the grossest forms of unthinking materialism to a spiritual perfection and an intelligent perception which will enable a man to become a member of the Kingdom of God.
5. It accounts for the differences among men and—in connection with the Law of Cause and Effect (called the Law of Karma in the East)—it accounts for differences in circumstances and attitudes to life.
6. It is the expression of the will aspect of the soul and is not the result of any form decision; it is the soul in all forms which reincarnates, choosing and building suitable physical, emotional and

mental vehicles through which to learn the next needed lessons.

7. The Law of Rebirth (as far as humanity is concerned) comes into activity upon the soul plane. Incarnation is motivated and directed from the soul level, upon the mental plane.

8. Souls incarnate in groups, cyclically, under law and in order to achieve right relations with God and with their fellowmen.

9. Progressive unfoldment, under the Law of Rebirth, is largely conditioned by the mental principle for "as a man thinketh in his heart, so is he." These few brief words need most careful consideration.

10. Under the Law of Rebirth, man slowly develops mind, then mind begins to control the feeling, emotional nature, and finally reveals the soul and its nature and environment to man.

11. At that point in his development, the man begins to tread the Path of Return, and orients himself gradually (after many lives) to the Kingdom of God.

12. When—through a developed mentality, wisdom, practical service and understanding—a man has learnt to ask nothing for the separated self, he then renounces desire for life in the three worlds and is freed from the Law of Rebirth.

13. He is now group conscious, is aware of his soul group and of the soul in all forms and has attained —as Christ had requested—a stage of Christlike perfection reaching unto the "Measure of the stature of the fulness of the Christ." (Eph. IV:13.)

Beyond this generalisation, no intelligent person will attempt to go. When Christ reappears, our knowledge will become more true and realistic; we shall know that we are eternally related to the souls of all men, and that we have a definite relationship to those who reincarnate with us, who are learning with us the same lessons and who are experiencing and experimenting with us. This proven and accepted knowledge will regenerate the very sources of our human living. We shall know that all our difficulties and all our problems are caused by our failure to recognise this fundamental Law, with its responsibilities and obligations; we shall then gradually learn to govern our activities by its just and restraining power. The Law of Rebirth embodies the practical knowledge which men need today to conduct rightly and correctly their religious, political, economic, communal and private lives and thus establish right relations with the divine life in all forms.

III. Revelation of the Mysteries of Initiation

Much that is here written and which is conveyed in these pages is in reality concerned with the appearance of the Kingdom of God—an appearance which can now take place because of three factors:

1. The growth of that Kingdom on Earth, and the thousands of people who recognise its laws and endeavour to live in accordance with its rules and spirit.
2. The fact that the signs of the time and the widespread need of humanity have evoked the Christ, and that He has decided to reappear.

THE TEACHINGS OF THE CHRIST

3. The invocative cry of humanity is ascending hourly to "the secret place of the Most High" and the Hierarchy plans to emerge when Christ appears and restores the rule of the Spirit on Earth. The hour for the restoration of the ancient Mysteries has arrived.

These facts have been widely given out, during the past two years, as the result of the cleansing of the Earth through the medium of the world war (1914-1945) and through the suffering to which humanity has been subjected (with an equally potent purifying effect, which will demonstrate later). It will then be possible for the Hierarchy, the Church of Christ hitherto invisible, to externalise itself and to function openly upon the physical plane. This will indicate a return to the situation which existed in Atlantean days when (to use Biblical symbology, Genesis Chaps. 2 and 3) God Himself walked among men; He talked with them and there was no barrier between the Kingdom of men and the Kingdom of God. Divinity was then present in physical form and the Members of the spiritual Hierarchy were openly guiding and directing the affairs of humanity, as far as man's innate freedom permitted. Now, in the immediate future, and on a higher turn of the spiral of life, this will again happen. The Masters will walk openly among men; the Christ will reappear in physical Presence. Another thing that will happen will be that the ancient Mysteries will be restored, the ancient landmarks will again be recognised—those landmarks which Masonry has so earnestly preserved and which have been hitherto securely embalmed in the Masonic rituals, waiting the day of restoration and of resurrection.

These ancient Mysteries were originally given to humanity by the Hierarchy and contain the entire clue to the evolutionary process, hidden in numbers, in ritual, in words and in symbology; these veil the secret of man's origin and destiny, picturing to him, in rite and ritual, the long, long path which he must tread, back into the light. They provide also (when rightly interpreted and correctly represented) the teaching which humanity needs in order to pass from darkness to Light, from the unreal to the Real and from death to Immortality. Any true Mason who understands, even if only to a slight degree, the significance of the three degrees of the Blue Lodge, and the implications of that in which he participates, will recognise the above three phrases for what they are, and will recognise the significance of the three degrees. I mention it here with Masonic purpose because it is closely related to the restoration of the Mysteries and has held the clue (down the ages) to that long awaited restoration, to the platform upon which the required teaching can be based and the structure which can express (when freed of its Jewish names and nomenclature, which are long out of date, though right three thousand years ago) the history of man's moving forward upon the Path of Return.

It is these Mysteries which Christ will restore upon His reappearance, thus reviving the churches in a new form, and restoring the hidden Mystery which they long have lost through their materialism. Masonry has also lost the true livingness it once possessed but, in its forms and rituals, the truth is preserved and can be recovered. This Christ will do. He will also revive these Mysteries in other ways; not all will seek the church or Masonry for the revitalising of their spiritual life. The true Mysteries will also reveal themselves through science and

THE TEACHINGS OF THE CHRIST

the incentive to search for them there will be given by the Christ. The Mysteries contain, within their formulas and teachings, the key to the science which will unlock the mystery of electricity—the greatest spiritual science and area of divine knowledge in the world, the fringes of which have only just been touched. Only when the Hierarchy is present visibly on Earth and the Mysteries of which the disciples of the Christ are the Custodians are given openly to the world, will the true secret and nature of electrical phenomena be revealed.

The Mysteries are, in the last analysis, the true source of revelation; it can only be when the mind and the will-to-good are closely fused and blended and are thus conditioning human behaviour that the extent of the coming revelation can be safely grasped. There are planetary energies and forces which men as yet cannot and do not control; they know nothing of them and yet upon them the life of the planet is dependent; they are also closely related to the despised psychic powers (today so stupidly approached and ignorantly used), yet these powers (when correctly assessed and used) will prove of enormous usefulness in *the sciences which the Mysteries will reveal*.

The Mystery of the Ages is, through the reappearance of the Christ, on the verge of revelation. Through the revelation of the soul that Mystery (which soul knowledge veils) will stand revealed. The Scriptures of the world have ever prophesied that, at the end of the age, we shall see the revelation of that which is secret and the emergence of that which has hitherto been concealed, into the light of day. As we know, our present cycle marks the end of the Piscean age; the next two hundred years will see the abolition of death or rather of our misconceptions as to death and the firm establishing of the fact of the soul's existence; the soul will then be known to be an entity and the motivating impulse and the spiritual force behind all manifested forms. The work of the Christ (two thousand years ago) was to proclaim certain great possibilities and the existence of great powers. His work when He reappears will be to prove the *fact* of these possibilities and to reveal the true nature and potency of man. The proclamation He made that we were all sons of God and own one universal Father will, in the near future, no longer be regarded as a beautiful, mystical and symbolic statement, but will be regarded as a proved scientific pronouncement. Our universal brotherhood and our essential immortality will be proven to be facts in nature.

The ground is being prepared at this time for the great restoration which the Christ will engineer. The world religions (including Christianity) and Masonry are today before the judgment seat of humanity's critical mind; the word has gone forth almost unanimously that both of them have failed in their divinely assigned tasks. It is realised everywhere that new life must be poured in, but this will take a new vision and a new approach to living conditions and this only the appearance of the Christ can teach and help us bring about. As an ancient Scripture says:

> "That which has been a mystery shall no longer be so, and that which has been veiled will now be revealed; that which has been withdrawn will emerge into the light and will then enhance that light and all men will see and together will rejoice. The time will come when destruction will have wrought its beneficent work; then men, through suffering, will seek that which they have discarded. In vain pursuit, they sought that which was near at hand and easy of at-

tainment. Possessed, they found that it proved an agency of death. Yet all the time, they sought for life, not death."

And the Christ will bring them life and life abundantly.

There is much talk these days concerning the mysteries of initiation. Every country is full of spurious teachers, teaching the so-called Mysteries, offering spurious initiations (usually at a cost and with a diploma) and misleading the people. Christ Himself taught that just before He came, this state of affairs would be found and that everywhere the false and the spurious would be proclaiming themselves. All this is, however, but indicative of His coming. The counterfeit ever guarantees the true. The talk, the discussions, the silly claim-making, the pseudo-occultism and the futile efforts to "take an initiation" (that undistinguished phrase which ignorant theosophical teachers have coined to express a deep spiritual experience) have been distinctive of the esoteric teaching ever since its modern inception in 1875. Then H. P. Blavatsky brought to the attention of the Western world the fact that great disciples and Masters of the Wisdom were present on the Earth, obedient to the guidance of the Christ. Later she deeply regretted doing this, as some of her papers, issued to her Esoteric Section, proclaimed. Yet what she did was all a part of the great plan and was no mistake. The interpretations and the excited reactions of the theosophists of her time were the mistake— a mistake which they have not yet acknowledged. This stupid reaction was aided and helped by the inquisitive nature of humanity itself, as well as by its aspiration which was undoubtedly aroused thereby. Men also, full of cupidity and commercial greed, exploited the theme and are still doing so.

The total effect of all these stupidities and errors of presentation has nevertheless been good. In all lands, men today are aware of the existence of the Masters and of the possibility offered and the opportunity presented to make *scientific* spiritual progress and thus become members of the Kingdom of God. This the churches had ignored and had—in the Victorian age particularly—looked upon science as an arch enemy.

All this flood of information about the mysteries of initiation—some of it indicative of a hidden truth, some of it the fabrications of an aspirational imagination and some commercially instigated—has definitely prepared humanity for the teaching it is believed Christ will give when again here with us in physical Presence.

Little as the orthodox Christian may care to admit it, the entire Gospel story in its four forms or presentations, contains little else except symbolic details about the Mysteries which are (as far as humanity is concerned) five in all. These Mysteries indicate, in reality, five important points in the spiritual history of an aspirant; they indicate also five important stages in the progress of human consciousness. This advance will become definite and clear in a manner not understood today, at some point during the Aquarian Age. Humanity, the world disciple (through its various groups all at various stages of unfoldment) will "enter into" new states of awareness and into new realms or spheres of mental and spiritual consciousness, during the next two thousand years.

Each age has left a reflection of a modern fivefold development upon it. Four ages have just passed away, astronomically speaking: Gemini, Taurus, Aries, and Pisces. Today Aquarius, the fifth age, is coming into power. In Gemini, its symbolical sign of the two pillars set its seal upon the Masonic Fraternity of the time

THE TEACHINGS OF THE CHRIST

and the two pillars of Jachin and Boaz—to give them their Jewish names which are, of course, not their real names—came into being approximately eight thousand years ago. Then came Taurus, the Bull, wherein Mithra came as the world Teacher and instituted the Mysteries of Mithras with an (apparent) worship of the Bull. Next followed Aries the Ram, which saw the start of the Jewish Dispensation which is of importance to the Jews and unfortunately of importance to the Christian religion, but of no importance to the untold millions in the other parts of the world; during this cycle came the Buddha, Shri Krishna and Sankaracharya; finally we have the age of Pisces the Fishes, which brought to us the Christ. The sequence of the Mysteries which each of the signs of the Zodiac embodies will be clarified for us by the Christ, because the public consciousness today demands something more definite and spiritually real than modern astrology, or all the pseudo-occultism so widely extant.

In the era which lies ahead, after the reappearance of the Christ, hundreds of thousands of men and women everywhere will pass through some one or other of the great expansions of consciousness, but the mass reflection will be that of the renunciation (though this does not mean that the masses will by any means take the fourth initiation); they will renounce the materialistic standards which today control in every layer of the human family. One of the lessons to be learnt by humanity at the present time (a time which is the ante-chamber to the new age) is how few material things are really necessary to life and happiness. The lesson is not yet learnt. It is, however, essentially one of the values to be extracted out of this period of appalling deprivations through which men are every day passing. The real tragedy is that the

Western Hemisphere, particularly the United States, will not share in this definite spiritual and vitalising process; they are at present too selfish to permit it to happen.

You can see, therefore, that initiation is not a ceremonial procedure, or an accolade, conferred upon a successful aspirant; neither is it a penetration into the Mysteries—of which the mysteries of Masonry are, as yet, only the pictorial presentation—but is simply the result of experiencing "livingness" on all three levels of awareness (physical, emotional and mental) and—through that livingness—bringing into activity those registering and those recording cells within the brain substance which have hitherto not been susceptible to the higher impression. Through this expanding area of registration or, if you prefer it, through the development of a finer recording instrument or responsive apparatus, the mind is enabled to become the transmitter of higher values and of spiritual understanding. Thus the individual becomes aware of areas of divine existence and of states of consciousness which are always eternally present but which the individual man was constitutionally unable to contact or to register; neither the mind, nor its recording agent, the brain, were able to from the angle of their evolutionary development.

When the searchlight of the mind is penetrating slowly into hitherto unrecognised aspects of the divine mind, when the magnetic qualities of the heart are awakening and becoming sensitively responsive to both the other aspects, then the man becomes able to function in the new unfolding realms of light, love and service. He is initiate.

These are the mysteries with which the Christ will deal; His acknowledged Presence with us and the presence of His disciples will make possible a far more rapid development than would otherwise be the case. The stimulation of the objective Hierarchy will be increasingly potent and the Aquarian Age will see so many of the sons of men accepting the great Renunciation that world effort will be on the same scale as the mass education of mankind in the Piscean Age. *Materialism as a mass principle will be rejected* and the major spiritual values will assume greater control.

The culmination of a civilisation, with its special note, quality and gifts to posterity, is significant of the reflection of the spiritual intent, and (through its massed populations) of one of the initiations. History will some day be based and written upon the record of the initiatory growth of humanity; prior to that, we must have a history which is constructed around the development of humanity under the influences of great and fundamental ideas. That is the next historical presentation.

The production of the culture of any given period is simply the reflection of the creative ability and the precise consciousness of the initiates of the time—those who knew they were initiate and were also conscious of admittance into direct relation with the Hierarchy. At present, we use neither of these two words, civilisation and culture, in their rightful sense or with their true meaning. Civilisation is *the reflection* in the mass of men of some particular cyclic influence, leading to an initiation. Culture is esoterically related to those within any era of civilisation who specifically, precisely and in full waking consciousness, through self-initiated effort, penetrate into those inner realms of thought activity which we call the creative world. These are the realms which are responsible for the outer civilisation.

The reappearance of the Christ is indicative of a closer relation between the outer and the inner worlds of thought. The world of meaning and the world of experience will be obviously blended through the stimulation of the advent of the Hierarchy and of its Head, the Christ. A tremendous growth of understanding and of relationships will be the major result.

IV. *The Dispelling of Glamour*

The word "glamour," the outstanding characteristic of the astral plane, has never been correctly employed and it is a pity that it was ever used in the early days of the esoteric teachings. The so-called "astral plane" is simply the name given to that sumtotal of sentient reactions, of feeling-responsiveness, and of emotional substance which man has himself so powerfully created and so successfully projected that he is today the victim of that which he has made. Eighty per cent of the teaching given about the astral plane is a part itself of the great delusion and a part also of that unreal world to which we refer when we pray the ancient prayer: "Lead us from the unreal to the Real." What is said about it has little basis in fact; it has, however, served a useful purpose as a field of experience in which we can learn to differentiate between the true and the untrue; it is an area also in which the aspirant can use the discriminating faculty of the mind—the great discloser of error and the eventual revealer of truth.

Once that "mind is in us which is also in Christ" (Phil. II:5), we shall find that the control of this emotional nature and this sentient area of consciousness (the astral plane, if you prefer the term!) becomes complete. Then this past sentient control and its entire area of influence no longer exists. It has no reality, except as a field of service and a realm in which men wander in despair and bewilderment. The greatest service a man

THE TEACHINGS OF THE CHRIST

can render his fellowmen is to free himself from the control of that plane by himself *directing its energies through the power of the Christ within*. He will then find that the self-centered forces and the energies of personal desire and of emotional love will be superseded by a living energy which can be sensed in a large way, though it cannot as yet be appropriated in its pure essence; this energy, we call the "love of God." It is that free-flowing, outgoing, magnetically attractive force which leads each pilgrim back to the Father's House. It is that force which stirs in the heart of humanity and finds expression through the medium of such great avatars as the Christ; which guides the mystical yearning found in each human being, and works through all movements that have for their objective the welfare of humanity, through philanthropic and educational tendencies of all kinds and through the instinctual motherhood found everywhere. But it is essentially a group sentiency, and only in the Aquarian Age, and as a result of the reappearance of the Christ, will its true nature reach correct understanding and the love of God be spread abroad in every human heart.

Of this world of glamour and illusion, Christ knew much, and in Himself demonstrated that true love could control it. Part of the three great temptations of the Christ in the wilderness was based upon the three aspects of world glamour: the *illusions* which the mind creates, the *glamour* of the emotional plane of experience and the *maze* of earthly circumstances. These all threatened to bewilder Him; He met each of them in turn with the enunciation of a clear-cut principle and not with the wordy arguments of an analytical mind; from that field of threefold experience He went forth to love, to teach and to heal. Christ is the great dispeller of world glamour when

He comes, and in this work the Buddha has previously prepared the way. The possibility of such a dispelling and dissipation is therefore definitely centred in the two Avatars, the Buddha and the Christ. One of the essential things at this time is to bring home to humanity and to the nations of the world the nature of the work undertaken by the Buddha and the Christ, and to re-emphasise the truths projected by Them into the arena of world thought. The work of the Lord of Light and of the Lord of Love must be presented anew to a needy world. In this connection, it might be said that some nations need to grasp the teaching of the Buddha which He enunciated in the *Four Noble Truths;* they must be brought to the realisation that the cause of all sorrow and woe is the misuse of desire—desire for that which is material and transitory. The United Nations need to learn to apply the Law of Love as enunciated in the life of Christ and to express the vitality of the truth that "no man liveth unto himself" (Rom. XIV:7) and no nation either; the goal of all human effort is loving understanding, prompted by a programme of love and right human relations for all mankind.

If the lives of these two great Teachers can be comprehended and Their teachings be wrought out in the lives of men anew today, in the world of human affairs, in the realm of human thinking and in the arena of political and economic intercourse, the present world order (which is so largely disorder) can be so modified and changed that a new world order and a new race of men can gradually come into being. World glamour will be dissipated and world illusion be dispelled.

Within the world of glamour—the world of the astral plane and of the emotions—appeared, centuries ago, a point of light; the Lord of Light, the Buddha, undertook to focus in Himself the illumination which would eventually make possible the dissipation of glamour. Within the world of illusion, the world of the mental plane, appeared the Christ, the Lord of Love Himself. He undertook to dispel illusion by drawing to Himself (by the attractive potency of love) the hearts of all men, and stated this determination in the words, "I, if I be lifted up, will draw all men unto Me." (John XII:32.)

The combined work of these two great Sons of God, concentrated through the world disciples and through Their initiates must and will inevitably shatter illusion and dispel glamour—the one by the intuitive recognition of reality by minds attuned to it, and the other by the pouring in of the light of the reason. The Buddha made the first planetary effort to dissipate world glamour; the Christ made the first planetary effort towards the dispelling of illusion. Their work must now be intelligently carried forward by a humanity wise enough to recognise its duty.

Men are being rapidly disillusioned and will consequently see more clearly. World glamour is being steadily removed from the ways of men. Those two developments have been brought about by the incoming new ideas, focussed through the world intuitives and released to the general public by the world thinkers. It is also largely aided by the unconscious, but none the less real, recognition by the masses of the true meaning of these *Four Noble Truths*. Disillusioned and deglamoured (if I may use such a term) humanity awaits the coming revelation. This revelation will be brought about by the combined efforts of the Buddha and the Christ. All that we can foresee or foretell anent that revelation is that some potent and far-reaching results will be achieved by the merging of light and love, and by the reaction of "lighted substance" to "the attractive power of love." I have here given a clue to the true understanding of the work of these Avatars—a thing hitherto quite unrealised. It might be added that when an appreciation of the meaning of the words "transfiguration of a human being" is gained, the realisation will come that when "the body is full of light" (Luke XI:36) then "in Thy light shall we see *light.*" (Ps. XXXVI:9.) This means that when the personality has reached a point of purification, of dedication and of illumination, then the attractive power of the soul, whose nature is love and understanding, can function, and fusion of these two will take place. This is what the Christ proved and demonstrated.

When the work of the Buddha (or of the embodied wisdom principle) is consummated in the aspiring disciple and his integrated personality, then the full expression of the work of the Christ (the embodied principle of love) can also be consummated; then both of these potencies—Light and Love—will find radiant expression in the transfigured disciple. What is true, therefore, of the individual is true also of humanity as a whole; today humanity (having reached maturity) can "enter into realisation" and consciously take part in the work of enlightenment and of spiritual, loving activity. The practical effects of this process will be the dissipation of glamour and the release of the human spirit from the thralldom of matter; it will produce also the dispelling of illusion and the recognition of the truth as it exists in the consciousness of those who are polarised in the awareness of the Christ.

This is necessarily no rapid process; it is an ordered and regulated procedure, sure in its eventual success but relatively slow also in its establishment and sequential process. This process was initiated upon the astral plane

THE TEACHINGS OF THE CHRIST

by the Buddha, and on the mental plane when Christ manifested on Earth. It indicated *the approaching maturity of humanity*. The process has been slowly gathering momentum as these two great Beings have gathered around Them Their disciples and initiates, during the past two thousand years. It has reached a point of intensive usefulness as the channel of communication between "the Centre where the Will of God is known," and the Hierarchy where the Love of God demonstrates has been opened and enlarged, and the contact between these two great centres and humanity has been more firmly established.

Thus thousands of intelligent men and women will be enabled to free themselves from all delusion and emotional control. The moment that *the hearts of men* are active, that moment sees the termination of emotional, solar plexus activity. That is a statement of fact; it is *the hearts of men* which respond to the call of Christ and it is those hearts which are becoming invocative today. The agonising emotional cycle through which humanity has passed during the past one hundred years, and the emotional tension in which men today live are also playing their part in fitting humanity to emerge into the realm of clear thought; this will mark a significant turning point in human history and will be one of the results of Christ's future scientific work (if I may use this term) with the hearts of men, bringing them into rapport with the Heart of God.

Because of the magnitude of this theme and the wide extent of the psychological area in which the mass of men now live, I cannot further enlarge. This field of experience and of trial is well known to all aspirants and is the battlefield of millions. The Christ within, as the Controller of the individual life, can bring that battle to an end; the aspirant can emerge clear sighted and unafraid. The appearance of the Christ among men will do the same thing for humanity as a whole, not in any vicarious sense but through the livingness of His Presence, stimulating the Christ principle in every human heart.

CHAPTER SIX

THE NEW WORLD RELIGION

THE world today is more spiritually inclined than ever before. This is said with a full realisation of the generally accepted idea that the world of men is on the rocks spiritually, and that at no time has the spiritual life of the race been at such a low ebb. This idea is largely due to the fact that humanity is not excessively interested in the orthodox presentation of truth, and that our churches are relatively empty and are under public indictment as having failed to teach humanity to live rightly. These affirmations are distressingly true, but the fact still remains that human beings everywhere are searching for spiritual release and truth, and that the truly religious spirit is more fundamentally alive than at any previous time. This is especially true of those countries which have suffered the most in the late world war (1914-1945). Countries, such as the United States and the neutral countries show, as yet, no sign of any real spiritual revival. The other countries are spiritually alive—not along orthodox lines but in a true search and a vital demand for light.

The religious spirit of humanity is today more definitely focussed upon Reality than has ever before been the case. The orthodox world religions are rapidly falling into the background of men's minds even whilst we are undoubtedly approaching nearer to the central spiritual Reality. The theologies now taught by the ecclesiastical organisation (both in the East and in the West) are crystallised and of relatively little use. Priests and churchmen, orthodox instructors and fundamentalists (fanatical though sincere) are seeking to perpetuate that which is old and which sufficed in the past to satisfy the enquirer, but which now fails to do so. Sincere but unenlightened religious men are deploring the revolt of youth from doctrinal attitudes. At the same time, along with all seekers, they are demanding a new revelation. They seek something new and arresting by which to attract the masses back to God; they fear that something must be relinquished, that new interpretations of old truths must be found, but fail to realise that a new outlook upon the truth (as it is in Christ) must be attained; they sense the approach of new, impending spiritual revelations but are apt to shrink back from their revolutionary effects. They ask themselves many questions and are assailed by deep and disturbing doubts. It is interesting here to note that the answers to these questions come (and will increasingly come), from two sources; the thinking masses, whose growing intellectual perception is the cause of the revolt from orthodox religion, and from that overshadowing source of truth and light which has unfailingly brought revelation down the ages. The answers will not come, as far as one can see, from any religious organisation, whether Asiatic or Western.

Some of these questions can be expressed as follows:

Why has the church been unable to arrest the overpowering expression of evil, as evidenced in the late world war?

Why has religion proved inadequate to the need of humanity?

Why have the so-called spiritual leaders of the religious world proved themselves incompetent to aid in the solution of the world problems?

Why, as exponents of the God of Love, have Christian teachers been unable to arrest the unparalleled growth of hate in the world today?

Why are the majority of such teachers so sectarian, separative and denominational in their approaches to truth? There is, however, a spiritual, open-minded minority.

Why do the young people refuse to go to church and lack interest to accept the doctrines presented for their belief?

Why is death and not life stalking the world today?

Why do so many new cults arise and sidetrack the people away from orthodox organisations of a religious nature?

Why does Mental Science, the Unity Movement and the New Thought presentation attract people away from the better established organisations? Note the use of the word "organisations"; it holds the key to the problem.

Why is there a growing emphasis upon the Eastern theologies, upon the various yogas, upon Buddhistic teachings and oriental faiths?

Why do such teachings as astrology, numerology and various magical rituals find so many adherents whilst the churches remain empty or are only attended by old people, the conservatives and reactionaries or by those who go there by force of habit, or desperate unhappiness?

What is wrong, finally, with our presentation of the spiritual realities and the truths of the ages?

Many answers can be given. The most important one is that *the presentation of divine truth,* as given by the churches in the West and by the teachers in the East, *has not kept pace with the unfolding intellect of the human spirit.* The same old forms of words and of ideas are still handed out to the enquirer and they do not satisfy his mind nor do they meet his practical need in a most difficult world. He is asked to give unquestioning belief but not to understand; he is told that it is not possible for him to comprehend and yet he is asked to accept the interpretations and the affirmations of other human minds who claim that they do understand and that they have the truth. He does not believe that their minds and their interpretations are any better than his. The same old formulas, the same old theologies and the same old interpretations are deemed adequate to meet man's modern needs and enquiries. They are not.

The church today is the tomb of the Christ and the stone of theology has been rolled to the door of the sepulchre.

There is, however, no point in attacking Christianity. *Christianity cannot be attacked; it is an expression—in essence, if not yet entirely factual—of the love of God, immanent in His created universe.* Churchianity has, however, laid itself wide open to attack, and the mass of thinking people are aware of this; unfortunately, these thinking people are still a small minority. Nevertheless, it is this thinking minority which (when it is a majority and it is today a rapidly growing one) will spell the doom of the churches and endorse the spread of the true teaching of the Christ. It is not possible that He has any pleasure in the great stone temples which churchmen have built, whilst His people are left without guidance or reasonable light upon world affairs; surely, He must feel (with an aching heart) that the simplicity which He taught and the simple way to God which He emphasised have disappeared into the fogs of theology (initiated by St. Paul) and in the discussions of churchmen throughout the centuries. Men have travelled far from the simplicity of thought and from the simple, spiritual life which the early

THE NEW WORLD RELIGION 141

Christians lived. Is it not possible that the Christ may regard the separative life of the churches and the arrogance of the theologians as wrong and undesirable—dividing (as they have) the world into believer and unbeliever, into Christian and heathen, into the so-called enlightened and the so-called benighted—and as contrary to all that He Himself held and believed when He said, "Other sheep I have which are not of this fold." (John X:16.)

It is not the evil rampant in the world today which is hindering the revelation and hindering the unfoldment of the spiritual life. That evil is the result of the misapprehension and the wrong orientation of the human mind, of the emphasis upon material things which ages of competitive activity have brought about; it rests upon the failure of the religious organizations throughout the world to preserve the truth in its purity and to avoid the fanatical idea that anyone's individual interpretation of truth must necessarily be the only and correct one. Theologians have fought (and with sincerity of intention) for forms of words which they believed were the only true and correct formulation of the divine idea, but Christ was forgotten behind the words; churchmen have expended effort and executive ability in raising funds for the building of stone edifices whilst God's children everywhere went hungry and unclothed and so lost their belief in divine love.

How can the need of humanity for spiritual guidance be met when the leaders of the churches are occupied with temporal concerns, when the emphasis is laid in the Roman Catholic, the Greek Orthodox and the Protestant Churches upon pomp and ceremonies, on great churches and stone cathedrals, upon gold and silver communion sets, on scarlet birettas, on jewelled vestments, and upon all the paraphernalia so cherished by the ecclesiastically minded? How can the starving children of the world—and of Europe in particular—be salvaged when pleas go out from Popes and Bishops for money to build cathedrals and erect more churches when the existent churches now stand empty? How can light shine again in the minds of men when churchmen keep the people in a state of fear unless they accept the old theological interpretations and the old ways of approaching God? How can the spiritual and intellectual needs of the people be met when the theological seminaries teach nothing new or appropriate to the day and age, but send out young men to guide humanity who are grounded only in the past interpretations. These young men enter upon their religious training and preparation for the ministry with high hopes and vision; they emerge with little hope, not much faith, but with a determination to "make good" and rise to prominence in the church.

The question arises whether Christ would be at home in the churches if He walked again among men. The rituals and the ceremonies, the pomp and the vestments, the candles and the gold and silver, the graded order of popes, cardinals, archbishops, canons and ordinary rectors, pastors and clergy would seemingly have small interest for the simple Son of God, Who—when on Earth—had not where to lay His head.

The presentation of religious truth in the past has blocked the growth of the religious spirit; theology has brought mankind to the very gates of despair; the delicate flower of the Christ life has been stunted and arrested in the dark caves of man's thinking; fanatical adherence to human interpretations has taken the place of Christian living; millions of books have obliterated the living words of Christ; the arguments and discussions of priests have put out the light which the Buddha brought, and the love of God as revealed by the life of Christ has been forgotten whilst men have quarrelled over meanings, over phrases and words. In the meantime, men have agonised, starved, suffered, demanded help and instruction and, unsatisfied, have lost faith.

Today everywhere people are ready for the light; they are expectant of a new revelation and of a new dispensation, and humanity has advanced so far on the way of evolution that these demands and expectations are not couched in terms of material betterment only, but in terms of a spiritual vision, true values and right human relations. They are demanding teaching and spiritual help along with the necessary requests for food, clothes and the opportunity to work and live in freedom; they face famine in large areas of the world and yet are registering (with equal dismay) the famine of the soul.

We are surely not in error if we conclude that this spiritual dismay and this spiritual demand have assumed a paramount place in the consciousness of the Christ. When He reappears and when His Church, hitherto invisible, appears with Him, what can They do to meet this demanding cry and this intensified attitude of spiritual perception with which They will be greeted. They see the picture whole. The cry of the Christian for spiritual help, the cry of the Buddhist for spiritual enlightenment, and the cry of the Hindu for spiritual understanding—along with the cries of all those who have faith or have no faith—must be met. The demands of humanity are rising to Their ears and the Christ and His disciples have no sectarian scruples, of that we may be sure. It is impossible to believe that They are interested in the views of the Fundamentalists or in the theories of the theologians upon the Virgin Birth, the Vicarious Atonement or the Infallibility of the Pope. Humanity is in desperate need and that need must be met; only great and fundamental principles of living, covering the past and the present and providing a platform for the future, will really meet that human invocation. The Christ and the spiritual Hierarchy will not come to destroy all that humanity has hitherto found "necessary to salvation," and all that has met its spiritual demand. When the Christ reappears, the non-essentials will surely disappear; the fundamentals of faith will remain, upon which He can build that new world religion for which all men wait. That new world religion *must* be based upon those truths which have stood the test of ages and which have brought assurance and comfort to men everywhere. These surely are:

1. *The Fact of God.*

First and foremost, there must be recognition of the fact of God. That central Reality can be called by any name that man may choose according to his mental or emotional bent, racial tradition and heritage, for it cannot be defined or conditioned by names. Human beings perforce always use names in order to express that which they sense, feel and know, both of the phenomenal and also of the intangible. Consciously or unconsciously, all men recognise God Transcendent and God Immanent. They sense God to be the Creator and the Inspiration of all that is.

The Eastern faiths have ever emphasised *God Immanent,* deep within the human heart, "nearer than hands and feet," the Self, the One, the Atma, smaller than the small, yet all-comprehensive. The Western faiths have presented *God Transcendent,* outside His universe, an Onlooker. God transcendent, first of all, conditioned men's concept of Deity, for the action of this transcendent God appeared in the processes of nature; later, in the Jewish

THE NEW WORLD RELIGION

dispensation, God appeared as the tribal Jehovah, as the soul (the rather unpleasant soul) of a nation. Next, God was seen as a perfected man, and the divine God-man walked the Earth in the Person of Christ. Today we have a rapidly growing emphasis upon God immanent in every human being and in every created form. Today, we should have the churches presenting a synthesis of these two ideas which have been summed up for us in the statement of Shri Krishna in *The Bhagavad Gita:* "Having pervaded this whole Universe with a fragment of Myself, I remain." God, greater than the created whole, yet God present also in the part; God Transcendent guarantees the plan for our world and is the Purpose, conditioning all lives from the minutest atom, up through all the kingdoms of nature, to man.

2. *Man's Relationship to God.*

The second truth to which all give allegiance—no matter what the faith—is that of man's essential relationship to God. Inherent in the human consciousness—inchoate often and undefined—is a sense of divinity. "We are all the children of God" (Gal. III:26); "One is our Father, even God," says the Christ and so say all the world Teachers and Avatars down the ages. "As He is, so are we in this world" (1 John IV:17) is another Biblical statement. "Closer is He than breathing, nearer than hands and feet," chants the Hindu. "Christ in us, the hope of glory" is the triumphant affirmation of St. Paul.

3. *The Fact of Immortality and of Eternal Persistence.*

Third, is the sense of persistence, of eternal life or of immortality. From this recognition, there seems to be no escape; it is as much a part of humanity's reaction as is the instinct of self-preservation. With that inner conviction, we face death and we know that we shall live again, that we come and we go and that we persist because we are divine and the controllers of our own destiny. We know that we have set ourselves a goal and that the goal is "Life more abundantly"—somewhere, here, there, and eventually everywhere.

The spirit in man is undying; it forever endures, progressing from point to point and stage to stage upon the Path of Evolution, unfolding steadily and sequentially the divine attributes and aspects. This truth involves necessarily the recognition of two great natural laws; the Law of Rebirth and the Law of Cause and Effect. The churches in the West have refused officially to recognise the Law of Rebirth and have thereby wandered into a theological impasse and into a cul-de-sac from which there is no possible exit. The churches in the East have over-emphasised these laws so that a negative, acquiescent attitude to life and its processes, based on continuously renewed opportunity, controls the people. Christianity has emphasised immortality but has made eternal happiness dependent upon the acceptance of a theological dogma: Be a true professing Christian and live in a somewhat fatuous heaven or refuse to be an accepting Christian, or a negative professional Christian, and go to an impossible hell—a hell growing out of the theology of *The Old Testament* and its presentation of a God, full of hate and jealousy. Both concepts are today repudiated by all sane, sincere, thinking people. No one of any true reasoning power or with any true belief in a God of love accepts the heaven of the churchmen or has any desire to go there. Still less do they accept the "lake that burneth with fire and brimstone" (Rev. XIX:20) or the everlasting torture to which a God of love is supposed to condemn all who do not believe in the theological interpretations of the Middle Ages, of the modern fundamentalists or of the unreasoning churchmen who seek—through doctrine, fear and threat—to keep people in line with the obsolete old teaching. The essential truth lies elsewhere. "Whatsoever a man soweth that shall he also reap" (Gal. VI:7) is a truth which needs re-emphasising. In these words, St. Paul phrases for us the ancient and true teaching of the Law of Cause and Effect, called in the Orient the Law of Karma.

The immortality of the human soul, and the innate ability of the spiritual, inner man to work out his own salvation under the Law of Rebirth, in response to the Law of Cause and Effect, are the underlying factors governing all human conduct and all human aspiration. These two laws no man can evade. They condition him at all times until he has achieved the desired and the designed perfection and can manifest on earth as a rightly functioning son of God.

4. *The Continuity of Revelation and the Divine Approaches.*

A fourth essential truth and one which clarifies all the planned work of the Christ is tied in with spiritual revelation and the need of man for God and of God for man. Never has Deity left Itself at any time without witness. Never has man demanded light that the light has not been forthcoming. Never has there been a time, cycle or world period when there was not the giving out of the teaching and spiritual help which human need demanded. Never did the hearts and minds of men go out towards God, but that divinity itself came nearer to man. The history of mankind is, in reality, the history of man's demand for light and for contact with God, and then the giving of light and the approach of God to man. Always the Saviour, the Avatar or the World Teacher issued forth from the secret place of the Most High and brought to man fresh revelation, fresh hope and a fresh incentive towards fuller spiritual living.

Some of these Approaches have been of a major nature, affecting humanity as a whole and some of them are of less importance, affecting only a relatively small part of mankind—a nation or a group. Those Who come as the Revealers of the love of God come from that spiritual centre to which the Christ gave the name "the Kingdom of God" (Matt. VI:33). Here dwell the "spirits of just men made perfect" (Heb. XII:23); here the spiritual Guides of the race are to be found and here the spiritual Executives of God's plan live and work and oversee human and planetary affairs. It is called by many names by many people. It is spoken of as the Spiritual Hierarchy, as the Abode of Light, as the Centre where the Masters of the Wisdom are to be found, as the Great White Lodge. From it come those who act as Messengers of the Wisdom of God, Custodians of the truth as it is in Christ, and Those Whose task is to save the world, to impart the next revelation, and to demonstrate divinity. All the world Scriptures bear witness to the existence of this centre of spiritual energy. This spiritual Hierarchy has been steadily drawing nearer to humanity as men have become more conscious of divinity and more fitted for contact with the divine.

Another great Approach of divinity and another spiritual revelation are now possible. A new revelation is hovering over mankind and the One Who will bring it and implement it is drawing steadily nearer to us. What

THE NEW WORLD RELIGION

this great approach will bring to mankind, we do not yet know. It will surely bring us as definite results as did all the earlier revelations and the missions of Those Who came in response to humanity's earlier demands. The World War has purified mankind. A new heaven and a new earth are on their way. What does the orthodox theologian and churchman mean when he uses the words "a new heaven"? May these words not signify something entirely new and a new conception as to the world of spiritual realities? May not the Coming One bring us a new revelation as to the very nature of God Himself? Do we yet know all that can be known about God? If so, God is very limited. May it not be possible that our present ideas of God, as the Universal Mind, as Love and as Will may be enriched by some new idea or quality for which we have as yet no name or word, and of which we have no slightest understanding. Each of the three present concepts of divinity—of the Trinity—were entirely new when first sequentially presented to the mind or consciousness of man.

For some years now the spiritual Hierarchy of our planet has been drawing nearer to humanity and its approach is responsible for the great concepts of freedom which are so close to the hearts of men everywhere. The dream of brotherhood, of fellowship, of world cooperation and of a peace, based on right human relations, is becoming clearer in our minds. We are also visioning a new and vital world religion, a universal faith which will have its roots in the past, but which will make clear the new dawning beauty and the coming vital revelation.

Of one thing we can be sure, this approach will, in some way—deeply spiritual, yet wholly factual—prove the truth of the immanence of God. The churches have emphasised and exploited the **extra-territoriality of Deity** and have posited the presence of a God Who is creating, sustaining and creatively active, but at the same time outside His Creation—an inscrutable onlooker. This type of transcendent Creator must be shown to be false and this doctrine must be countered by the manifestation of God in man, the hope of glory. It is this surely that the expected Approach will demonstrate; it will prove also the close relationship between God Transcendent and that in "Him we live and move and have our being," because, "having pervaded this entire Universe with a fragment of Himself, He *remains.*" God is immanent in the forms of all created things; the glory which shall be revealed is the expression of that innate divinity in all its attributes and aspects, its qualities and powers, through the medium of humanity.

On the fact of God and of man's relation to the divine, on the fact of immortality and of the continuity of divine revelation, and upon the fact of the constant emergence of Messengers from the divine centre, the new world religion will be based. To these facts must be added man's assured, instinctive knowledge of the existence of the Path to God and of his ability to tread it, when the evolutionary process has brought him to the point of a fresh orientation to divinity and to the acceptance of the fact of God Transcendent and of God Immanent within every form of life.

These are the foundational truths upon which the world religion of the future will rest. Its keynote will be *Divine Approach.* "Draw near to Him and He will draw near to you" (James IV:8) is the great injunction, emanating in new and clear tones from Christ and the spiritual Hierarchy at this time.

The great *theme* of the new world religion will be the recognition of the many divine approaches and the continuity of revelation which each of them conveyed; the

THE NEW WORLD RELIGION

task ahead of the spiritually minded people of the world today is to prepare humanity for the imminent and (perhaps) the greatest of all the Approaches. The *method* employed will be the scientific and intelligent use of Invocation and Evocation and the recognition of their tremendous potency.

Man invokes divine Approach in various ways: by means of the inchoate, voiceless appeal or invocative cry of the masses and also by the planned, defined invocation of the spiritually oriented aspirants, the intelligently convinced worker, disciple and initiate,—by all, in fact, who form the New Group of World Servers.

The science of invocation and evocation will take the place of what we now call "prayer" and "worship." Be not disturbed by the use of the word "science." It is not the cold and heartless intellectual thing so oft depicted. It is in reality the intelligent organisation of spiritual energy and of the forces of love, and these, when effective, will evoke the response of spiritual Beings Who can again walk openly among men, and thus establish a close relation and a constant communication between humanity and the spiritual Hierarchy.

In order to clarify, it might be said that Invocation is of three kinds: there is, as stated above, the massed demand, unconsciously voiced, and the crying appeal, wrung from the hearts of men in all times of crisis such as the present. This invocative cry rises ceaselessly from all men living in the midst of disaster; it is addressed to that power outside themselves which they feel can and should come to their help in their moment of extremity. This great and wordless invocation is rising everywhere today. Then there is the invocational spirit, evidenced by sincere men as they participate in the rites of their religion and take advantage of the opportunity of united worship and prayer to lay their demands for help before God. This group, added to the mass of men, creates a huge body of invocative applicants and at this time, their massed intent is in great evidence and their invocation is rising to the Most High. Then, lastly there are the trained disciples and aspirants of the world who use certain forms of words, certain carefully defined invocations and who—as they do this—focus the invocative cry and the invocative appeal of the other two groups, giving it right direction and power. All these three groups are, consciously or unconsciously, swinging into activity at this time and their united effort guarantees a resultant evocation.

This new invocative work will be the keynote of the coming world religion and will fall into two parts. There will be the invocative work of the masses of the people, everywhere, trained by the spiritually minded people of the world (working in the churches whenever possible under an enlightened clergy) to accept the fact of the approaching spiritual energies, focussed through Christ and His spiritual Hierarchy, and trained also to voice their demand for light, liberation and understanding. There will also be the skilled work of invocation as practised by those who have trained their minds through right meditation, who know the potency of formulas, mantrams and invocations and who work consciously. They will increasingly use certain great formulas of words which will later be given to the race, just as the Lord's Prayer was given by the Christ, and as the New Invocation has been given out for use at this time by the Hierarchy.

This new religious science for which prayer, meditation and ritual have prepared humanity, will train its people to present—at stated periods throughout the year— the voiced demand of the people of the world for relation-

THE NEW WORLD RELIGION 153

ship with God and for a closer spiritual relation to each other. This work, when rightly carried forward, will evoke response from the waiting Hierarchy and from its Head, the Christ. Through this response, the belief of the masses will gradually be changed into the conviction of the knowers. In this way, the mass of men will be transformed and spiritualised, and the two great divine centres of energy or groups—the Hierarchy and Humanity itself—will begin to work in complete at-one-ment and unity. Then the Kingdom of God will indeed and in truth be functioning on earth.

It will be apparent to you that it is only possible to indicate the broad general outlines of the new world religion. The expansion of the human consciousness which will take place as a result of the coming Great Approach will enable humanity to grasp not only its relation to the spiritual life of our planet, the "One in Whom we live and move and have our being," but will also give a glimpse of the relation of our planet to the circle of planetary lives, moving within the orbit of the Sun and the still greater circle of spiritual influences which contact our system as it pursues its orbit in the Heavens (the twelve constellations of the zodiac). Astronomical and astrological investigation has demonstrated this relationship and the influences exerted but there is still speculation and much foolish claiming and interpretation. Yet the churches have ever recognized this and the Bible has testified to it. "The stars in their courses fought against Sisera" (Judges V.20). "Who can withstand the sweet influences of the Pleiades?" (Job XXXVIII.31). Many other passages bear out this contention of the Knowers. Many church festivals are fixed by reference to the moon or a zodiacal constellation. Investigation will prove this to be the case and when the ritual of the new world religion is universally established, this will be one of the important factors considered.

The establishing of certain major festivals in relation to the Moon and in a lesser degree to the zodiac will bring about a strengthening of the spirit of invocation and the resultant inflow of evoked influences. The truth lying behind all invocation is based upon the power of thought, particularly in its telepathic nature, rapport and aspect. The unified, invocative thought of the masses and the focussed, directed thought of the New Group of World Servers constitute *an outgoing stream of energy.* This will reach telepathically those spiritual Beings Who are sensitive and responsive to such impacts. Their evoked response, *sent out as spiritual energy,* will in turn reach humanity after having been stepped down into thought energy and in that form will make its due impact upon the minds of men, convincing them and carrying inspiration and revelation. Thus has it ever been in the history of the spiritual unfoldment of the world and the procedure followed in writing the world Scriptures.

Secondly, the establishing of a certain uniformity in the world religious rituals will aid men everywhere to strengthen each other's work and enhance powerfully the thought currents directed to the waiting spiritual Lives. At present, the Christian religion has its great festivals, the Buddhist keeps his different set spiritual events, and the Hindu has still another list of holy days. In the future world, when organised, all men of spiritual inclination and intention everywhere will keep the same holy days. This will bring about a pooling of spiritual resources, and a united spiritual effort, plus a simultaneous spiritual invocation. The potency of this will be apparent.

Let me indicate the possibilities of such spiritual events, and attempt to prophesy the nature of the coming world-

THE NEW WORLD RELIGION 155

wide Festivals. There will be three such major Festivals each year, concentrated in three consecutive months and leading, therefore, to a prolonged annual spiritual effort which will affect the remainder of the year. These will be:

1. *The Festival of Easter.* This is the Festival of the risen, living Christ, the Teacher of all men and the Head of the Spiritual Hierarchy. He is the Expression of the love of God. On this day the spiritual Hierarchy, which He guides and directs, will be recognised and the nature of God's love will be emphasised. This Festival is determined always by the date of the first Full Moon of spring and is the great Western and Christian Festival.

2. *The Festival of Wesak.* This is the Festival of the Buddha, the spiritual Intermediary between the highest spiritual centre, Shamballa, and the Hierarchy. The Buddha is the expression of the wisdom of God, the Embodiment of Light and the Indicator of the divine purpose. This will be fixed annually in relation to the Full Moon of May, as is at present the case. It is the great Eastern Festival.

3. *The Festival of Goodwill.* This will be the Festival of the spirit of humanity—aspiring towards God, seeking conformity with the will of God and dedicated to the expression of right human relations. This will be fixed annually in relation to the Full Moon of June. It will be a day whereon the spiritual and divine nature of mankind will be recognised. On this Festival for two thousand years the Christ has represented humanity and has

stood before the Hierarchy and in the sight of Shamballa as the God-Man, the leader of His people and "the Eldest in a great family of brothers" (Romans VIII:29). Each year at that time He has preached the last sermon of the Buddha, before the assembled Hierarchy. This will, therefore, be a festival of deep invocation and appeal, of a basic aspiration towards fellowship, of human and spiritual unity, and will represent the effect in the human consciousness of the work of the Buddha and of the Christ.

These three Festivals are already being kept throughout the world, though they are not as yet related to each other and are a part of the unified spiritual Approach of humanity. The time is coming when all three Festivals will be kept throughout the world and by their means a great spiritual unity will be achieved and the effects of the Great Approach, so close to us at this time, will be stabilised by the united invocation of humanity throughout the planet.

The remaining full moons will constitute lesser festivals but will be recognised to be also of vital importance. They will establish the divine attributes in the consciousness of man, just as the major festivals establish the three divine aspects. These aspects and qualities will be arrived at and determined by a close study of the nature of a particular constellation or constellations influencing those months. For instance, Capricorn will call attention to the first initiation, the birth of the Christ in the cave of the heart, and indicate the training needed to bring about that great spiritual event in the life of the individual man. I give this one instance to you in order to indicate the possibilities for spiritual unfoldment that

THE NEW WORLD RELIGION 157

could be given through an understanding of these influences and in order to revivify the ancient faiths by expanding them into their larger undying relationships.

Thus, the twelve annual festivals will constitute a revelation of divinity. They will present a means of bringing about relationship, first of all, during three months with the three great spiritual Centres, the three expressions of the divine Trinity. The minor festivals will emphasise the inter-relation of the Whole, thus lifting the divine presentation out of the individual and the personal, into that of the universal divine Purpose; the relationship of the Whole to the part and of the part to that Whole will be thereby fully expressed.

Humanity will, therefore, invoke the spiritual power of the Kingdom of God, the Hierarchy; the Hierarchy will respond, and God's plans will then be worked out on earth. The Hierarchy, on a higher turn of the spiral will invoke the "Centre where the Will of God is known," thus invoking the Purpose of God. Thus will the Will of God be implemented by Love and manifested intelligently; for this mankind is ready, and for this the Earth waits.

To sum up therefore: on the basis of the fundamental truth already recognised the new world religion will be built.

The definition of religion which will in the future prove of greater accuracy than any yet formulated by the theologians might be expressed as follows:

> *Religion is the name given to the invocative appeal of humanity and the evocative response of the greater Life to that cry.*

It is, in fact, the recognition by the part of its relationship to the Whole, plus a constantly growing demand for increased awareness of that relation; it draws forth the recognition of the Whole that the demand has been made. It is the impact of the vibration of humanity—oriented specifically to the Great Life of which it feels itself a part—upon that Life and the responsive impact of that "All-surrounding Love" upon the lesser vibration. It is only now that the impact of the human vibration can dimly be sensed in Shamballa; hitherto its most potent activity has only reached the Hierarchy. Religion, the science of invocation and evocation as far as humanity is concerned, is the approach (in the coming New Age) of a mentally polarised humanity. In the past, religion has had an entirely emotional appeal. It concerned the relation of the individual to the world of reality, of the seeking aspirant to the sought-for divinity. Its technique was the process of fitting oneself for the revelation of that divinity, of achieving a perfection which would warrant that revelation, and of developing a sensitivity and a loving response to the ideal Man, summarised, for present day humanity, in the Christ. Christ came to end the cycle of this emotional approach which had existed since Atlantean days; He demonstrated in Himself the visioned perfection and then presented to humanity an example—in full manifestation—of every possibility latent in man *up to that time*. The achieving of the perfection of the Christ-consciousness became the emphasised goal of humanity.

Today, slowly, the concept of a world religion and the need for its emergence are widely desired and worked for. The fusion of faiths is now a field for discussion. Workers in the field of religion will formulate the universal platform of the new world religion. It is a work of loving synthesis and will emphasise the unity and the fellowship of the spirit. This group is, in a pronounced sense, a

THE NEW WORLD RELIGION

channel for the activities of the Christ, the world Teacher. The platform of the new world religion will be built by many groups, working under the inspiration of the Christ.

Churchmen need to remember that the human spirit is greater than all the churches and greater than their teaching. In the long run, that human spirit will defeat them and proceed triumphantly into the Kingdom of God, leaving them far behind unless they enter as a humble part of the mass of men. Nothing under heaven can arrest the progress of the human soul on its long pilgrimage from darkness to light, from the unreal to the real, from death to immortality and from ignorance to wisdom. If the great organised religious groups of churches in every land, and composing all faiths do not offer *spiritual* guidance and help, humanity will find another way. Nothing can keep the spirit of man from God.

The churches in the West need also to realise that basically there is only one Church, but it is not necessarily only the orthodox Christian institution. God works in many ways, through many faiths and religious agencies; this is one reason for the elimination of non-essential doctrines. By the emphasising of the essential doctrines and in their union will the fullness of truth be revealed. This, the new world religion will do and its implementation will proceed apace, after the reappearance of the Christ.

CHAPTER SEVEN

PREPARATION FOR THE REAPPEARANCE OF THE CHRIST

The Needed Preparation
The Work of the New Group of World Servers

IF the general premise and theme of all that has been here written is accepted, the question necessarily arises: What should be done to hasten this reappearance of the Christ? and also: Is there anything that the individual can do, in the place where he is and with the equipment, opportunities and assets of which he stands possessed? The opportunity is so great and the need for definite and explicit spiritual help is so demanding that—whether we like it or not—we are faced with a challenge. We are confronted with the choice of acceptance and consequent responsibility, or with rejection of the idea and the consequent realisation that we are not concerned. What we decide, however, in this time and period, will definitely affect the remainder of our life activity, for we shall either throw what weight or aid we can on the side of the invocation of the Christ and in preparation for His return, or we shall join the ranks of those who regard the whole proposition as an appeal to the gullible and the credulous, and possibly work to prevent men being deceived and taken in by what we have decided is a fraud. Herein lies our challenge. It will take all that we have of a sense of values and all that we can give to a specialised intuitive research to meet it. We may then realise that this promised reappearance is in line with general re-

PREPARATION FOR THE CHRIST 161

ligious belief and the major hope left in the minds of men which can bring true relief to suffering humanity.

To those who accept the possibility of His reappearance and who are willing to admit that history can again repeat itself, there are three questions which can be asked—the answers to which are strictly individual. These are:

1. How can I personally meet this challenge?
2. What can I specifically *do?*
3. What are the steps which I should take and where are those who will take them with me?

What is written here and in the following pages is essentially for those who accept the fact of Christ, recognise the continuity of revelation and are willing to admit the possibility of His return.

The complexities and the difficulties of this postwar period are very great. The closer a man may be to the source of spiritual light and power, the more difficult is his problem, for human affairs at this time seem so far away from this divine possibility. He will need all that he has of patience, understanding and goodwill. At the same time, the clearer will be his recognition of the facts. There are inner and outer problems which must be solved; there are inner and outer possibilities which can be made factual. As the spiritually-minded man faces both these inner and outer possibilities and events, it is easy to register a sense of complete frustration; he longs to help but knows not what to do; his grasp of the menacing difficulties, his analysis of his resources and of those with whom he will have to work, and his clarity of perception as to the forces ranged against him (and on a much larger scale against the Christ) will make him inclined to ask: "What is the use of any effort which I can make? Why not let the forces of good and evil fight it out alone? Why not permit the pressure of the evolutionary current—eventually and at long last—to bring cessation to the world fight and usher in the triumph of the good? Why attempt anything *now?*"

These are natural and wholesome reactions. The poverty and starvation of the millions in Europe and elsewhere, the fear of Russia (warranted or unwarranted), the greed of the capitalistic forces of the world, the selfishness of labour, the aggressiveness of the Zionists, claiming as their own a land which has not been theirs for more than fifteen hundred years, the plight of the Jews in Europe, the desperation of the little man in every country who sees no security or hope anywhere, the work of the churches as they endeavour to restore the old order and rule which (over the centuries) has saved the world from little, and the lack of any clear voice or leadership in any country—all these things make the average man feel the futility of all effort. The problem seems too big, too terrible, and he himself seems too small and helpless.

Nevertheless, the mass of straight goodness and vision in the world is enormous and the amount of clear, humanitarian thinking is unbounded; it is in the hands of the masses of good little men and the millions of right thinking people in every land that the salvation of the world lies and by them the preparatory work for the Coming of the Christ will be done. Numerically, they are adequate to the task and need only re-assurance and wise coordination to prepare them for the service required,

PREPARATION FOR THE CHRIST

before the reappearance of the Christ becomes possible. The problems confronting us should be faced *with courage,* with truth and understanding; as well as with the willingness to speak factually, with simplicity and with love in the effort to expose the truth and clarify the problems which must be solved. The opposing forces of entrenched evil must be routed before He for Whom all men wait, the Christ, can come.

The knowledge that He is ready and anxious publicly to appear to His loved Humanity only adds to the sense of general frustration, and another very vital question arises: For what period of time must we endure, struggle and fight? The reply comes with clarity: He will come unfailingly when a measure of peace has been restored, when the principle of sharing is at least in process of controlling economic affairs, and when churches and political groups have begun to clean house. Then He can and will come; then the Kingdom of God will be publicly recognised and will no longer be a thing of dreams and of wishful thinking and orthodox hope.

People are prone to ask the question as to why the Christ does not come—in the pomp and ceremony which the churches ascribe to the event—and, by His coming, demonstrate His divine power, prove convincingly the authority and the potency of God, and thus end the cycle of agony and distress. The answers to this are many. It must be remembered *that the main objective of the Christ will not be to demonstrate power but to make public the already existent Kingdom of God.* Again, when He came before He was unrecognised, and is there any guarantee that this time it would be different? You may ask why would He not be recognised? Because men's eyes are blinded with the tears of self-pity and not of contrition; because the hearts of men are still corroded with a selfishness which the agony of war has *not* cured; because the standards of value are the same as in the corrupt Roman Empire which saw His first appearance, only then these standards were localised and not universal as they are today; because those who could recognise Him and who hope and long for His coming are not willing to make the needed sacrifices, and thus ensure the success of His advent.

The advanced thinking, the success of the many esoteric movements and above all, the marvels of science and the wonder of the many humanitarian movements, indicate no divine frustration but growth of spiritual understanding; the forces of the spirit are unconquered. These aspects of human behaviour indicate the wonder of the divinity which is in man and the success of the divine plan for humanity. Divinity, however, awaits the expression of man's *free will;* his intelligence and his growth in goodwill are already being expressed.

Therefore, another answer to the question posited is that Christ and the spiritual Hierarchy never—no matter how great the need or important the incentive—infringe upon the divine right of men to make their own decisions, to exert their own free will and to achieve freedom by fighting for freedom—individually, nationally and internationally. When true freedom covers the earth, we shall see the end of tyranny—politically, religiously and economically. I am not here referring to modern democracy as a condition which meets the need, for democracy is at present a philosophy of wishful thinking and an unachieved ideal. I refer to that period which will surely come in which an *enlightened people* will rule; these people will not tolerate authoritarianism in any church or totalitarianism in any political system; they will not accept or permit the rule of any body of men who undertake

PREPARATION FOR THE CHRIST 165

to tell them what they *must* believe in order to be saved or what government they *must* accept. When the people are told the truth and when they can freely judge and decide for themselves, we shall then see a much better world.

It is not essential or necessary that all these desirable objectives should be accomplished facts upon Earth before Christ again moves amongst us. It is, however, necessary that this attitude to religion and politics is generally regarded as desirable and that steps have been successfully taken in the direction of right human relations. It is along these lines that the New Group of World Servers and all men of goodwill are working, and their first effort must be to offset the widespread sense of frustration and individual futility.

That which will offset the sense of frustration and futility and provide likewise the needed incentive towards the re-building of the new world will be the belief in the essential divinity of humanity, in the evolutionary proof (which a little study quickly provides) that mankind has steadily moved onward in wisdom and knowledge, and a wide inclusiveness, plus the development of that state of mind which will base itself upon belief in the veracity of the historical records which bear witness to the many advents at crucial times in human affairs, and to the many world Saviours—of Whom the Christ was the greatest. A right and constructive attitude must also be based on an innate recognition of the existence of the Christ and of His Presence with us at all times; it must be grounded in the knowledge that the war—with all its unspeakable horrors, its cruelties and its cataclysmic disasters—was but the broom of the Father of all, sweeping away all obstructions in the path of His returning Son. It would have been wellnigh impossible to prepare for the coming in the face of the pre-war conditions. Upon these facts the New Group of World Servers must, today, take their stand. They must recognise the obstructing factors, but must also refuse to be frustrated by them; they must be aware of the hindrances (many of them financial and based on material greed, on ancient tradition and national prejudices). They must then employ such skill in action and such business acumen that these hindrances will be overcome; they must walk cleareyed through world difficulties and pass unscathed and successful through the midst of all frustrating factors.

There are two major factors which condition the present opportunity; these can be regarded as so completely hindering that unless they are removed, there will be a long delay before Christ can return. They are:

1. The inertia of the average Christian or spiritually-minded man in every country—Eastern or Western.
2. The lack of money for the work of preparation.

We will keep these themes simple and down on the level at which most people work and think today. Let us be intensely practical and force ourselves to look at *conditions as they are,* thus arriving at a better knowledge of ourselves and of our motives.

1. The Inertia of the Average Spiritually-Minded Man.

The average spiritually-minded person, man of goodwill, or disciple is constantly aware of the challenge of the times and the opportunity which spiritual events may offer. The desire to do good and to accomplish spiritual ends are ceaselessly gnawing away within his consciousness. No one who loves his fellowmen, who has a dream of seeing the Kingdom of God materialise on earth, or who is conscious of the awakening—slow though it may be—of the masses to the higher spiritual values but is thoroughly dissatisfied. He realises that what he contributed of help to these desirable objectives is little indeed. He knows that his spiritual life is a side issue; it is something which he keeps carefully to himself and which he is frequently afraid to mention to his nearest and his dearest; he tries to dovetail his spiritual efforts into his ordinary, outer life, struggling to find time and opportunity for it in a gentle, futile and innocuous manner. He finds himself helpless before the task of organising and rearranging his affairs so that the spiritual way of living may dominate; he searches for alibis for himself and eventually rationalises himself so successfully that he ends by deciding that he is doing the best he can in the given circumstances. The truth is that he is doing so little that probably one hour out of the twenty-four (or perhaps two) would cover the time given to the Master's work; he hides behind the alibi that his home obligations prevent his doing more and does not realise that—given tact and loving understanding—his home environment can and must be the field in which he triumphs; he forgets that *there exist no circumstances in which the spirit of man can be defeated* or in which the aspirant cannot meditate, think, talk and prepare the way for the coming of the Christ, provided he cares enough and knows the meaning of sacrifice and silence. *Circumstances and environment offer no true obstacle to the spiritual life.*

Perhaps he hides behind the alibi of poor health and frequently behind that of imaginary ills. He gives so much time to the care of himself that the hours which could be given to the Master's work are directly and seriously curtailed; he is so pre-occupied with feeling tired, or tending a cold, or with fancied heart difficulties that his "body consciousness" steadily develops until it eventually dominates his life; it is then too late to do anything. This is particularly the case with people who have reached their fiftieth year or over. It is an alibi which it is hard not to use, for many feel tired and ailing and this, as the years go by, is apt to get worse.

The only cure for this creeping inertia is to ignore the body and take your joy in the livingness of service. I speak here not of definite disease or of serious physical liabilities; to these right care and attention must be duly given; I speak to the thousands of ailing men and women who are pre-occupied with taking care of themselves, and so waste hours of the time which could be given to the service of humanity. Those who are seeking to tread the Path of Discipleship should release those many hours spent in needless self-care into the service of the Hierarchy.

Still another alibi, leading to inertia, is *the fear* people have of speaking about the things of the kingdom of God to others; they are afraid of being rebuffed, or of being thought peculiar, or of intruding. They, therefore, preserve silence, lose opportunity and never discover how ready people are for the discussion of realities, for the comfort and hope which the thought of Christ's return can bring, or for the sharing of spiritual light. This is essentially a form of spiritual cowardice but is so widespread that it is responsible for the loss of millions of hours of world service.

There are other alibis, but those above noted are the most common; the release of the majority of people from these hindering conditions would bring to the service of the Christ so many hours and so much overtime endeavour that the task of those who admit no alibis would be greatly lightened and the coming of the Christ would be much nearer than it is today. To the rhythm of life under which the Christ and the spiritual Hierarchy operate, and which vibrates in harmony with human need and spiritual response, we are not called. We are, however, called to demonstrate the quality of spiritual activity and to refuse to hide behind alibis. It is essential that all spiritual people recognise that in the place where they now are, among the people who are their associates and with the psychological and physical equipment with which they are endowed, *they can and must work*. There is no possible coercion or undue pressure exerted in the service of the Hierarchy. The situation is clear and simple.

There are, at the present time, three great activities going on:—

First, the activity to be felt in the "centre where the will of God is known," that will-to-good which has carried all creation on toward a greater glory and a steadily deepening, intelligent responsiveness. This today is creatively endeavouring to bring in the new world order, the order of the Kingdom of God under the *physical* supervision of the Christ. This might be regarded as the externalisation of the spiritual Hierarchy of our planet. Of this, the return of the Christ to *visible* activity will be the sign and the symbol.

Secondly, the critical activity which is conditioning the spiritual Hierarchy, from the Christ Himself down to the lowest aspirant to be found on the periphery of that "centre where the love of God" has full play. *There,* it is fully realised that (in the words of St. Paul) "the whole creation groaneth and travaileth in pain together until now, waiting for the manifestation of the Sons of God" (Romans VIII:22). It is for that manifestation They now prepare, these "Sons of God Who are the Sons of Men;" it is for this coming forth to outer active service that They are already—one by one—entering into outer activity upon the physical plane. They are not recognised for what They are, but They go about the Father's business, demonstrating goodwill, seeking to enlarge the horizon of humanity, and thus prepare the way for the One Whom They serve, the Christ, the Master of all the Masters and the Teacher alike of angels and of men.

Thirdly, there is humanity itself, "the centre which we call the race of men"—a centre at present full of chaos, turmoil and confusion, a humanity full of pain, bewilderment, disturbance, yet mentally aware of infinite possibilities, emotionally fighting for that plan which seems to them to be the best, but with no sense of coherency or any realisation that it must be the *"one world for the one humanity."* They desire simply emotional peace, security in which to live and work, and a vision of a future which will satisfy some inchoate sense of divine persistence. They are physically ill, deprived for the most part of the essentials of normal wholesome living, wracked with the sense of financial insecurity and—consciously or unconsciously—invoking the Father of all on behalf of themselves and of the rest of the world.

The solution is to be found in the reappearance of the Christ. This is the ascertained will of God, and to it the Scriptures of the world testify; it is the desire of Christ Himself and of His disciples, the Masters of the Wisdom; it is the unrealised demand of peoples in all lands. Where there is this unification of purpose, this uniformity of spiritual intention and of realised demand, then there is only one thing which can arrest His reappearance and that is the failure of mankind to prepare the world stage for that stupendous event, to "prepare the Way of the Lord, make His paths straight" (Matthew III:2), to

PREPARATION FOR THE CHRIST 171

familiarise the people everywhere with the idea of His coming, and bring about the required measure of peace on earth—a peace based upon right human relations.

It is surely needless here to deal with the theme of the preparation which the individual should make within himself as he prepares for the work to be done. Men have had the principles of right spiritual conduct presented to them for centuries, though largely because good conduct will lead them to a good heaven, the aim has been basically selfish. The little prayer which says, "Lord God Almighty! Let there be peace on earth and let it begin with me," sums up all the requirements for those who seek to work in preparation for the coming of the Christ, if to it is added the development of a sound intelligence and the practice of an organised life. But today the motive shifts from the concept of personal salvation (which is assumed or taken for granted), and the preparation required is that of working, with strength and understanding, to bring about right human relations—a broader objective. There we have a motive which is not self-centred but which ranges each individual worker and humanitarian on the side of the spiritual Hierarchy, putting him in touch with all men of goodwill. We come now to the second of the major hindrances: the lack of financial support for the workers of the Christ.

2. *Lack of Financial Support for the Work of the Christ.*

This is perhaps the major difficulty, and it appears to many at times to be an insuperable one. It involves the problem of true financial trusteeship and the deflection of adequate sums of money into channels which will definitely aid in the work of preparation for the return of the Christ. It is closely tied up with the problem of right human relations.

The problem is, therefore, a peculiarly hard one, for the spiritual workers of the world have not only to train people *to give* (according to their means) but, in many cases, they have—first of all—to provide them with a motive so magnetic in its appeal that they must perforce give. They have also to provide the trust, foundation or organisation through which the given money may be administered. This presents them with a most impressively difficult task. The impasse which at present exists is not based only upon the novelty of raising funds in preparation for the return of the Christ, but it is based also upon the trained selfishness of the majority who own the world's wealth and who—even if they do give—do so because it fosters prestige and indicates financial success. Necessarily, there are exceptions to this but they are relatively few.

Generalising, therefore, and over-simplifying the subject, we can assume that money finds it way into four main channels of expenditure:

1. Into the myriad homes in the world in the form of wages, salaries or inherited wealth. All this is at present most unevenly balanced, producing extreme riches or extreme poverty.
2. Into great capitalistic systems and monopolies which are found as towering structures in most lands. Whether this capital is owned by the government, or by a municipality, or by a handful of wealthy men or by the great labour unions matters not. Little of it is spent in the betterment of human living or for the inculcation of those values which lead to right human relations.

PREPARATION FOR THE CHRIST

3. Into the churches and religious groups throughout the world. Here (again speaking in general terms and at the same time recognising the existence of a spiritually-minded minority) the money is deflected into the material aspects of the work, into the multiplying and preservation of ecclesiastical structures, into salaries and general overhead, and only a percentage of it really goes into the teaching of the people, into a living demonstration of the simplicity "as it is in Christ," and into the spreading of the fact of His return—for centuries a definite doctrine of the churches. That return has been anticipated down the ages, and might have occurred ere now had the churches and religious organisations everywhere done their duty.

4. Into philanthropic, educational and medical work. All of this has been exceedingly good and greatly needed and the debt of the world to the public-spirited men who have made these institutions possible is great indeed. All of this has been a step in the right direction and an expression of the divine will-to-good. It is, however, frequently money misused and misdirected and the values developed have been largely institutional and concrete. They have been limited by the separative tenets of the donors, or the religious prejudices of those who control the disbursement of the funds. In the quarrelling over ideas, religious theories and ideologies, the true assistance of the One Humanity is overlooked.

The fact remains that had the directing agencies (through whose hands the money of the world is channelled) any true vision of the spiritual realities, of the one humanity and the one world, and had their objective been the stimulation of right human relations, the mass of men everywhere would be responding to a future possibility very different from the present one; we would not be faced as we are today with the expenditures—running into countless billions—necessitated by the need to restore *physically,* not only the physical bodies of countless millions of men, but entire cities, transportation systems and centres responsible for the reorganisation of human living.

Equally, it can be said that if the spiritual values and the spiritual responsibilities attached to money (in large quantities or in small) had been properly appreciated and taught in homes and schools, we would not have had the appalling statistics of the money spent, prior to the war in every country in the world (and spent today in the Western Hemisphere) on candy, liquor, cigarettes, recreation, unnecessary clothes and luxuries. These statistics run into hundreds of millions of dollars every year. A fraction of this money, necessitating the minimum of sacrifice, would enable the disciples of the Christ and the New Group of World Servers to prepare the way for His coming and to educate the minds and hearts of men in every land in right human relations.

Money—as with all else in human living—has been tainted by selfishness and grabbed for selfish individual or national ends. Of this, the World War (1914-1945) is the proof, for, although there was much talk of "saving the world for democracy" and "fighting a war to end war," the main motive was self protection and self-preservation, the hope of gain and the satisfaction of ancient hatreds, and the regaining of territory. The years which have elapsed since the war have proved this to be so. The United Nations is unfortunately perforce occupied with rapacious demands from all sides, with the angling

PREPARATION FOR THE CHRIST 175

of the nations for position and power, and for the possession of the natural resources of the earth—coal, oil, etc., and also with the underground activities of the great Powers and of the capitalists which they all create.

Yet all the time, the one humanity—no matter what the place of residence, what the colour of the skin, or what the religious belief—is clamouring for peace, justice and a sense of security. This, the right use of money and a realisation on the part of many of their financial responsibility (a responsibility based on the spiritual values) would rapidly give them. With the exception of a few great farsighted philanthropists and of a mere handful of enlightened statesmen, churchmen and educators, this sense of financial responsibility is to be found nowhere.

The time has now come when money must be revaluated and its usefulness channelled into new directions. The voice of the people must prevail, but it must be a people educated in the true values, in the significances of a right culture and in the need for right human relations. It is, therefore, essentially a question of right education and correct training in world citizenship—a thing that has not yet been undertaken. Who can give this training? Russia would gladly train the world in the ideals of communism, and would gather all the money in the world into the coffers of the proletariat, eventually producing the greatest capitalistic system the world has ever seen; Great Britain would gladly train the world in the British concepts of justice and fair play and world trade, and would do it more correctly than any other nation because of vast experience but always too with an eye to profit. The United States would also gladly undertake to force the American brand of democracy upon the world, using her vast capital and resources in so doing, and gathering into her banks the financial results of her widespread financial dealings, preserving them safely by the threat of the atomic bomb and the shaking of the mailed fist over the rest of the world. France will keep Europe in a state of unrest as she seeks to regain her lost prestige and garner all she can from the victory of the other allied nations. Thus the story goes—each nation fighting for itself, and all rating each other in terms of resources and finance. In the meantime, humanity starves, remains uneducated, and is brought up on false values and the wrong use of money. Until these things are in process of being righted, the return of the Christ is not possible.

In the face of this disturbing financial situation— what is the answer to the problem? There are men and women to be found in every land, every government, every church and religion, and every educational foundation who have the answer. What hope is there for them and for the work with which they have been entrusted? How can the people of the world, the men of goodwill and of spiritual vision help? Is there anything they can do to change the thinking of the world in regard to money, thus deflecting it into channels where it will be more correctly used? The answer must be found.

There are two groups who can do much: those already using the financial resources of the world, if they will catch the new vision and also see the handwriting on the wall which is bringing the old order down in destruction, and, secondly, the mass of the good, kindly, people in all classes and spheres of influence.

Men of goodwill and of spiritual inclination must reject the thought of their relative uselessness, insignificance and futility, and realise that now (in the critical and crucial moment that has come) they *can* work potently. The Forces of Evil *are* defeated, though not yet "sealed" behind the door where humanity can put them

PREPARATION FOR THE CHRIST

and which *The New Testament* foretold would happen. Evil is seeking every avenue available for a new approach but—and this we can say with confidence and insistence—the little people of the world, enlightened and selfless in their viewpoint, *exist in sufficient numbers to make their power felt*—if they will. There are millions of spiritually-minded men and women in every country who, when they come to the point of approaching in mass formation this question of money, can *permanently re-channel it*. There are writers and thinkers in all lands who can add their powerful help, and who will, if correctly approached. There are esoteric students and devoted church people to whom appeal can be made for aid in preparing the way for the return of Christ, particularly if the aid required is the expenditure of money and time for the establishing of right human relations and the growth and spread of goodwill.

A great campaign to raise money is not demanded, but the selfless work of thousands of apparently unimportant people is required. I would say that the most needed quality is *courage;* it takes courage to put aside diffidence, shyness and the dislike of presenting a point of view, particularly a point of view connected with money. It is here that the majority fail. It is relatively easy today to raise money for the Red Cross, for hospitals and for educational institutions. It is exceedingly difficult to raise money for the spread of goodwill, or to secure the right use of money for forward looking ideas, such as the return of the Christ. Therefore, I say that *the first prerequisite is Courage*.

The second requirement for the workers of the Christ is to make those sacrifices and arrangements which will enable them to give to the limit of their capacity; there must not be simply a trained ability to present the subject, but each worker must practice what he preaches. If, for instance, the millions of people who love the Christ and seek to serve His cause gave at least a tiny sum of money each year, there would be adequate funds for His work; the needed trusts and spiritually-minded trustees would then automatically appear. The difficulty is not with the organising of the money and work; it lies with the seeming inability of people to give. For one reason or another, they give little or nothing, even when interested in such a cause as that of the return of Christ; fear of the future or the love of purchasing, or the desire to give presents, or failure to realise that many small sums mount up into very large sums—all these things militate against financial generosity and the reason always seems adequate. Therefore, *the second pre-requisite is for everyone to give as they can.*

Thirdly, the metaphysical schools and the esoteric groups have given much thought to this business of directing money into channels which appeal to them. The question is often asked: Why do the Unity School of thought, the Christian Science Church, and many New Thought movements always manage to accumulate the required funds whilst other groups, and particularly the esoteric groups, do not? Why do truly spiritual workers seem unable to materialise what they need? The answer is a simple one. Those groups and workers who are the closest to the spiritual ideal are as a house divided against itself. Their main interest is on abstract, spiritual levels and they have not apparently grasped the fact that the physical plane, when motivated from the spiritual levels, is of equal importance. The large metaphysical schools are focussed on making *a material demonstration,* and so great is their emphasis and so one-pointed is their approach that they get what they demand; they have to learn that

PREPARATION FOR THE CHRIST 179

the demand and its answer must be the result of spiritual purpose, and that that which is demanded must not be for the use of the separated self or for a separative organisation or church. In the new age which is upon us, prior to the return of the Christ, the demand for financial support must be for the bringing about of right human relations and goodwill, and not for the growth of any particular organisation. The organisations so demanding must work with the minimum of overhead and central plant, and the workers for the minimum yet reasonable salary. Not many such organisations exist today, but the few now functioning can set an example which will be rapidly followed, as the desire for the return of Christ grows. Therefore *the third pre-requisite is the service of the one humanity.*

The *fourth pre-requisite must be the careful presentation of the cause* for which the financial support is required. People may have the courage to speak, but an intelligent presentation is of equal importance. The major point to be emphasised in the preparatory work for the return of Christ is the establishing of right human relations. This has already been started by men of goodwill all over the world, under their many names.

We come now to the *fifth pre-requisite: a vital and sure belief in humanity as a whole.* There must be no pessimism as to the future of mankind or distress over the disappearance of the old order. "The good, the true and the beautiful" is on its way, and for it mankind is responsible, and not some outer divine intervention. Humanity is sound and rapidly awakening. We are passing through the stage where everything is being proclaimed from the housetops—as Christ stated would be the case—and as we listen to or read of the flood of filth, crime, and sensual pleasure or luxury buying, we are apt to be discouraged; it is wise to remember that it is wholesome for all this to come to the surface and for us all to know about it. It is like the psychological cleansing of the subconscious to which individuals submit themselves; it presages the inauguration of a new and better day.

There is work to do and the men of goodwill, of spiritual instinct, and of truly Christian training must do it. They must inaugurate the era of the use of money for the spiritual Hierarchy, and carry that need into the realms of invocation. Invocation is the highest type of prayer there is, and a new form of divine appeal which a knowledge of meditation has now made possible.

There is naught to add in the way of an appeal for funds, courage or understanding. If the courage of the Christ, as He faces return to this physical, outer world, if the need of humanity for right human relations and the sacrificing work of the disciples of the Christ are not enough to fire you and to energise you and those whom you can reach, there is nothing that can be said which will be of any use.

We have considered the need of preparation for the coming of the Christ and some of the basic requirements which will arise as people brace themselves for the needed activity, including the raising of the necessary finances to carry forward the preparatory work. The individual worker has, first of all, to decide if his incentive and spiritual expectancy is adequate to the task ahead. Only that is of importance which provides a needed momentum for action, and only that worker will be equal to the task who has a vision of sufficient clarity to enable him to work with understanding and sincerity. He must discover that it *is* possible for him to play his part in the furthering of the divine Plan. The fact of Christ and the genuine

PREPARATION FOR THE CHRIST

possibility of His reappearance must become important motivating factors in his consciousness. He looks around for those with whom he may work, and who have the same spiritual objectives as he has. In this way and in due time, he finds that there exists on Earth a well organised and integrated group to which can be given the name of the New Group of World Servers. He finds that they are everywhere, and are functioning in every country and in all the organised religious groups and all other groups, dedicated to the well-being of humanity and to preparing the way for the return of the Christ.

This is primarily a group which, while working on the outer plane of daily, physical living, yet preserves a close, inner, spiritual integration with the centre of energy from which it can draw all that is needed for active, spiritual work. The group provides a field of service for all who are seeking service-expression; it also provides a rallying point for all who are willing to be tried out, and a place where their motives and persistence can be tested, prior to a steady unfoldment of spiritual opportunity. He is thus freed for ever enlarging areas of service.

The New Group of World Servers provides essentially a training ground and a field of experience for those who hope to grow in spiritual stature and to fit themselves to be the active, directed disciples of the Christ. The appearance of this group on Earth at this time is one of the indications of the success of the evolutionary process, as applied to humanity. This method of work—the use of human beings as agents to carry forward the work of salvation and of world uplift—was initiated by the Christ Himself; He worked with men very frequently through others, reaching humanity through the medium of His twelve Apostles, regarding Paul as substituting for Judas Iscariot. The Buddha tried the same system but the relation of His group was, in the first instance, to Him and not so much to the world of men. Christ sent His Apostles out into the world to feed the sheep, to seek, to guide and to become "fishers of men." The relation of the disciples of the Christ was only secondarily to their Master but primarily to a demanding world; that attitude still controls the Hierarchy, yet with no loss of devotion to the Christ. What the Buddha had instituted symbolically and in embryo became factual and existent under the demands of the Piscean Age.

In the age into which we are now emerging, the Aquarian Age, this mode of group work will reach a very high point of development, and the world will be saved and reconstructed *by groups* far more than by individuals. In the past we have had world saviours—Sons of God Who have given to men a message which brought an increase of light to the people. Now, in the fullness of time, and through the processes of evolution, there is emerging a group who will bring salvation to the world and who (embodying groups ideas and emphasising the true meaning of the Church of Christ) will so stimulate and energise the minds and souls of men that the new age will be ushered in by an outpouring of the Love, Knowledge and Harmony of God Himself, as well as by the reappearance of the Christ in Whom all these three faculties of divinity will be embodied.

Religions in the past have been founded by a great soul, by an Avatar, and by an outstanding spiritual personality. The stamp of their lives and words and teaching has been set upon the race and has persisted for many centuries. What will be the effect of the message of a group Avatar or world Saviour? What will be the potency of the work of a group of knowers of God, enunciating truth and banded together subjectively in the great work

PREPARATION FOR THE CHRIST 183

of saving the world? What will be the effect of the mission of a group of world Saviours, all Knowers of God in some degree, who supplement each other's efforts, reinforce each other's message, and constitute an organism through which the spiritual energy and principle of spiritual life can make their presence felt in the world, under the direction of the Christ in Visible Presence?

Such a body now exists, with its members in every land. Relatively they are few and far between, but steadily their numbers are increasing, and increasingly their message will be felt. In them is vested a spirit of construction; they are the builders of the new age; to them is given the work of preserving the spirit of truth, and the reorganising of the thoughts of men so that the racial mind is controlled and brought into that meditative and reflective condition which will permit it to recognise the next unfoldment of divinity, which Christ will inaugurate.

For the last ten years, this New Group of World Servers has been reorganised and revitalised; the knowledge of its existence is spreading all over the world. It is today a group of men and women of every nation and race and of all religious organisations and humanitarian movements who are fundamentally oriented towards the Kingdom of God or who are in process of thus orienting themselves. They are disciples of the Christ, working consciously and frequently unconsciously for His reappearance; they are spiritual aspirants, seeking to serve and make real the Kingdom of God on Earth; they are men of goodwill and intelligence who are trying to increase understanding and right human relations among men. This group is divided into two major divisions:—

1. A group composed of the disciples of the Christ who are consciously working with His plans, and

of those who, instructed by them, are consciously and voluntarily cooperating. In this latter category we can find ourselves if we so desire, and if we are willing to make the necessary sacrifices.

2. A group composed of aspirants and world conscious men and women, who are working unconsciously under the guidance of the spiritual Hierarchy. There are many such, particularly in high places today, who are fulfilling the part of destroyers of the old form or of builders of the new. They are not conscious of any inner synthetic plan, but are selflessly occupied in meeting world need as best they may, with playing parts of importance in national dramas, or with working persistently in the field of education.

The first group is in touch with the spiritual Hierarchy to some extent and to a large extent where true disciples are concerned; its members work under spiritual inspiration. The second group is in closer touch with the masses of men; it works more definitely under the inspiration of ideas. The first group is occupied with the Plan of the Christ as far as its members can grasp its essentiality, whilst the second group works with the new concepts and hopes which are emerging in the consciousness of mankind, as men begin subjectively and often unconsciously to respond to the preparations for the coming of the Christ. Steadily and as a result of the work of the New Group of World Servers, humanity is awakening to the possibilities ahead.

The awakening of the intelligentsia in all countries to the recognition of *humanity* is a prelude to the establishment of brotherhood. The unity of the human family is recognised by man, but before that unity can take

PREPARATION FOR THE CHRIST

form in constructive measures, it is essential that more and more of the thinking men and women throughout the world should break down the mental barriers existing between races, nations and types; it is essential that the New Group of World Servers should itself repeat in the outer world that type of activity which the Hierarchy expressed when it developed and materialised the New Group of World Servers. Through the impression and expression of certain great ideas, men everywhere must be brought to the understanding of the fundamental ideals which will govern the new age. This is the major task of the New Group of World Servers.

As we study and learn to recognise the New Group of World Servers in all its branches and spheres of activity—scattered all over the world and embracing true and earnest workers and humanitarian people in every nation, every religion and every organisation of humanitarian intent—we shall awaken to the realisation that there is on Earth today a body of men and women whose numbers and range of activities are entirely adequate to bring about the changes which will enable the Christ to walk again amongst us. This will come about if they care enough, are ready enough to make the needed sacrifices and are willing to sink their national, religious and organisational differences in the carrying out of those forms of service which will reconstruct the world. They must educate the race of men in a few simple and basic essentials and familiarise humanity with the thought of the reappearance of the Christ and the externalisation of the Kingdom of God. Their work will be largely to summarise and make effective the work of the two Sons of God: the Buddha and the Christ.

The success of the work of the New Group of World Servers is inevitable; they have made much headway during the past ten years; the inner integration of that part of the group which works in close touch with Christ and the spiritual Hierarchy is such that the outer success is guaranteed. They provide a channel through which the light, love and power of the Kingdom of God can reach the more exoteric workers.

Therefore, let us realise that all spiritually inclined men and women, all who seek and work for the establishing of right human relations, all who practise goodwill and truly endeavour to love their fellowmen are an integral part of the New Group of World Servers and that their major task at this time is to prepare the way for the reappearance of the Christ.

Let me emphatically here state that the major method with which we can concern ourselves and the most potent instrument in the hands of the spiritual Hierarchy is the spreading of goodwill and its fusion into a united and working potency. I prefer that expression to the words "the organisation of goodwill." Goodwill is today a dream, a theory, a negative force. It should be developed into a fact, a functioning ideal, and a positive energy. This is our work and again we are called to cooperate.

The task before the New Group of World Servers is great, but it is not an impossible task. It is engrossing, but as it constitutes an imposed life pattern, it can be worked out in every aspect of a man or woman's normal, daily life. Yet at the same time, we are called to abnormal living, and to the shouldering of a definite responsibility.

CONCLUSION

THE call for preparation for the reappearance of the Christ has gone out; the call to world salvage has sounded forth, and today spiritually-minded men everywhere and disciples of the Christ are assembling all over the world. It is not an assembling upon the physical plane but a profound subjective and spiritual happening. Even those with only a faint glimmer of understanding as to what the call truly signifies are responding, and asking for the opportunity to help, and for guidance as to what they may do.

Today, therefore, we wait for the new Appearing. The Christ is universally expected, and in this spirit of expectancy comes the antidote to the spirit of fear and horror which has descended upon our unhappy planet. Humanity today looks in two directions: towards the devastated Earth and the agonised hearts of men; it also looks towards the Place from whence the Christ will come, which they symbolically call "heaven." Where there is the same expectancy, where there is uniformity of testimony and of prediction, and where all the indications of "the time of the end" are with us, is it not reasonable to believe that a great event *is* in process of taking place? If, in the midst of death and destruction, there is to be found a living faith (and there is such a faith everywhere) and a burning zeal which pierces through the darkness to the centre of light, does that not warrant the assumption that this faith and this zeal are founded on a deep intuitive knowledge. May it not be a divine fact that "faith is *the substance* of things hoped for, the *evidence* of things not seen?" (Hebrews XI:1.)

Humanity in all lands today awaits the Coming One—no matter by what name they may call Him. The Christ is sensed as on His way. The second coming is imminent and, from the lips of disciples, mystics, aspirants, spiritually-minded people and enlightened men and women, the cry goes up, "Let light and love and power and death fulfill the purpose of the Coming One." These words are a demand, a consecration, a sacrifice, a statement of belief and a challenge to the Avatar, the Christ, Who waits in His high place until the demand is adequate and the cry clear enough to warrant His appearance.

One thing it is most necessary to have in mind. It is *not* for us to set the date for the appearing of the Christ or to expect any spectacular aid or curious phenomena. If our work is rightly done, He will come at the set and appointed time. How, where or when He will come is none of our concern. Our work is to do our utmost and on as large a scale as possible to bring about right human relations, for His coming depends upon our work.

All of us can do something to bring the present terrible world situation to an end and to better conditions: the least of us can play our part in inaugurating the new era of goodwill and understanding. It must be realised, however, that it is no millenium for which we work but that our main objective is, at this time, twofold:

1. To break the ancient and evil rhythms and establish a new and better one. It is here that *time* is a paramount factor. If we can delay the crystallisation of the ancient evils which produced the world war, and arrest the reactionary forces in every nation, we shall be making way for that which is new and opening the door to the activities

of the New Group of World Servers in every land—that group which is the agent of the Christ.
2. To fuse and blend the united aspiration and longing of the people everywhere so that the sound of humanity's demand may be strong enough to reach the spiritual Hierarchy.

This will require sacrifice, understanding and a deep love of our fellowmen. It will also require intelligence and wisdom and a practical grasp of world affairs. As the work goes forward in the establishing of right human relations (which is the basic world need) and as the method of so doing—goodwill—is developed, the Christ and His disciples will steadily approach closer to mankind. If the initial premise is accepted that He *is* on His way, then all spiritually oriented people and the disciples and aspirants of the world will inevitably work—but the premise must be accepted if the incentive is to prove adequate. It is with this thought that we look into the future. The fiat of the Lord has gone forth; Christ stands attentive to the demand of humanity. That demand is rising and mounting every day and "'in such an hour as you think not, *He will come.*"

The sons of men are one, and I am one with them.
I seek to love, not hate;
I seek to serve and not exact due service;
I seek to heal, not hurt.

Let pain bring due reward of light and love.
Let the soul control the outer form,
And life, and all events,
And bring to light the Love
That underlies the happenings of the time.

Let vision come and insight.
Let the future stand revealed.
Let inner union demonstrate and outer cleavages be
      gone.
Let love prevail.
Let all men love.

Training for new age discipleship is provided by the *Arcane School*. The principles of the Ageless Wisdom are presented through esoteric meditation, study and service as a *way of life*.

*Write to the publishers
for information.*

INDEX

A

Affirmation of Christ, 29
Ancient of Days. *See* Lord of the World.
April, 1945, Full Moon, 90-91
Approaches, divine, 147-156
Aquarian —
  energy, inflow, 85-86
  World Teacher, 82-83, 86
Aquarian Age —
  builders, 98
  duties of Christ, 71, 72, 83, 98
  forerunner, 79-88, 86
  gift to humanity, 80
  group work, 182
  influence, 81-82
Aquarius, symbolism, 80
Aries, Age —
  and Jewish Dispensation, 127
  influence, 106
  worship, 79, 81
Ascension initiation, 54
Aspect —
  Life, expression, 85
  Will, dynamic pull, 72
  Will, forces of reconstruction, 93
Aspects, three divine, development in mankind, 88
Aspirant, spiritual history, 126
Astronomical ages, five, 126-127
Atlantis, truths, 103
Authoritarianism disallowed, 164-165
Avatar —
  coming, causes, 8, 10, 11
  definitions, 6, 7, 8-9, 11
  descent, precipitation, 9
  group, effect, 182-183
  manifestation, 11
  of Love, 12
  task, 11
Avatar of Synthesis —
  aid to Christ, 76-78, 82, 97, 101, 111
  aid to humanity, 93-94
  energy, type, 93
Avatars —
  approaches to humanity.
    See Approaches.
  demand for, responses, 41
  doctrine, 5-14
  incentives, 7
  See also Saviours; Teachers, world.

B

"Babes in Christ", definition, 87
Baptism initiation, 86
Bhagavad Gita —
  quotations, 4, 36, 145
  teacher, 107
Birth —
  new, initiation.
    See Initiation, first.
  of Christ in heart, 86
Blavatsky, H. P., spread of fact of Masters, 125
Brain —
  relation to mind, 128
  substance, activation, 128
Bread, symbolism, 80
Brotherhood —
  dream, clarification, 149
  establishment, prelude, 184
  of man, foundation, 21
  of man, recognition, 41
  universal, proof, 124
Buddha, Lord —
  aid to Christ, 100-101, 106, 111
  and Christ, combined efforts, 133
  characteristic, predominant, 97
  cycle, 127
  dissipation of glamour and illusion, 132-135
  Festival, 155
  Four Noble Truths, 20, 106
  future work, 96-97
  higher service, 40, 82, 96-97

knowledge re: Christ, 99
last sermon, 156
light, extinction by buddhists, 142
love-wisdom, 92
mission, 61
new truths, 12
Noble Eightfold Path, 20-21
Noble Middle Way, 90
presence at Wesak Festival, 45, 46, 96
quotation, 58
readiness, 38, 39
relation to Christ, 100-101, 106, 107
teaching, 105-107
truths, 66
vestures, 100-101
work —
   future, 93, 96-97
   results, 10-11, 12, 93, 96, 181-182
   strengthening, 185
Buddha-Spirit of Peace-Avatar of Synthesis Triangle, 111
Buddhism, revival, 20-21
Bull, astrological sign. *See* Taurus.

C

Carpenter, symbolism, 97-98
Centre, solar plexus, activity, termination, 135
Christ —
  activities, channel, 159
  activities, limitation, 18
  affirmation, 29
  aid —
    of Avatar of Synthesis, 76-78, 82, 97, 101
    of Buddha, 100-101
    to Avatar of Synthesis, 93-94
  and Buddha, combined efforts, 133-134
  approach, Signs, 44
  attention, shift, 18
  awareness of potency of will, 27
  challenge, 188
  consciousness. *See* Christ-consciousness.
  crises, 27, 28, 68-79
  crucifixion, symbolism, 97-98
  decisions in 1945, 23-25, 30, 69, 71, 72, 78, 82, 86

demonstration, 134
departure for Jerusalem, meaning, 28
departure from planet, 57
development, evolutionary, 70
disciples. *See* Disciples of Christ.
dispelling of glamour, 130-135
duties, 71, 72, 83
emphasis on teaching of Buddha, 108
endeavour, new fields, 18
energies to be expressed, 62
example, 108
existence, recognition, 165
expansion of consciousness, 25-27
focal point and transmitting Agent for five energies, 98-99
followers, 110-111
forerunner group, 44
functions, two new, 83
in Gethsemane. *See* Gethsemane.
in temple, interpretation, 27-28
in visible Presence, direction of group work, 183
inauguration of new era, 23
influence of Triangle, 111
initiation of disciples, 87
initiations, 39, 54, 55
invocation of, 22
knowledge, 25, 26, 27
lifted up, interpretation, 29-30
Light and life, 58
love, 9, 12, 36-37
love-wisdom, 92
manifestation, painful ordeal, 109
message, response to, 114
mission, 61, 62
monadic, realisation, 27-30
nationality and religion, 19
nature, 67
new fields of endeavour, 18
opportunity, 61, 62
orientation, 28
overshadowing by Spirit of Peace, 74-75
overshadowing of disciples, 48, 83
physical supervision, 169
Plan, work with, 184
point of —
  climax, 69

INDEX

crisis, 28, 68, 69, 78
decision, 69
emergence, 68
tension, 68, 69, 73, 78
powers possible of achievement by man, 49-53
preparation for —
  by —
    acceptance of basic principles, 109
    aspirants and men of goodwill, 62, 162, 167
    Buddha, 107
    Christ Himself, 66
    conquest of evil, 163
    deflecting money into proper channels, 176, 177, 178, 179, 180
    development of spiritual recognition, 19
    disciples, 10, 63, 67, 84, 108, 174
    establishing order, 109
    establishing right human relations, 30-31, 163, 164-165, 171, 177, 179
    Hierarchy, 58, 79, 169-170
    invocation and evocation, 151
    New Group of World Servers, 84, 165-166, 174, 181-186
    removal of hindrances, 164-166, 168-169, 171-172, 174-180
    right education, 175
    spiritual forces, 19-20, 22, 23, 30, 47
    spiritual people, 151, 180-181
    world peace, 59, 163, 171
  questions regarding, 160-162
  workers, requirements, 171
presence —
  acknowledged, result, 128
  continuous, 43-44, 46, 165
  physical, 46, 121
problems, 67, 90
purpose, 158, 163
reaction to His own destiny, 26-27
readiness, 38, 39, 95
reappearance —
  causation, 8, 10, 12-13
  circumstances, 58, 59, 110
  connotation, 69
  dependence upon humanity, 66
  expectancy, conditions, 5-6, 10, 37-44, 62, 187
  hastening, 23
  indication, 129
  major effect, 110-111
  motives, 72
  one world, 16
  physical, 169
  results, 13-14, 120, 122, 123, 131
  stimulation, results, 130
  success factors, 73
  timing, 43, 66-67, 72, 100, 109-110, 113
  unification of purpose, 170
recognition, lack, causes, 163-164
relation to —
  Aquarian Age, 79-88
  Buddha, 100-101, 108, 155
  New Age, 182
release of energy, 88-95
renunciation, 26
respect for free will, 164
response to spiritual demands, 143-144
responses in two directions, 67
rhythm of life, 169
risen, proof of transfiguration of lower nature, 30
spirit, desertion by Christian Church, 140, 141, 142-143
suffering, 55
sword, 110, 111
tasks, 55, 56-57
teachings —
  departure from, 140-141
  distortion, 43, 48, 49, 54, 56-57, 63-65, 70
  future, spread, 140
  regarding —
    human soul, 107
    initiation, 120-130
    Law of Rebirth, 115-120
    renunciation, 23
    resurrection life, 23
    right human relations, 108, 110-115
    service, 107-108

INDEX

temptations in wilderness, 131
test, 55
tragedy, causes, 99-100
training by, 55
training of, 97, 98, 99
unification of East and West,
  95-101
unique occasion, 15-35
use of Invocation, 34
visible activity, 169
visions, 25, 26
will. *See* Will.
with you always, interpretation, 29
work —
  future —
    66, 93, 94, 122-123, 124,
    135, 136
  in Aquarian Age. *See*
    Aquarian Age.
  in Palestine, 99, 124, 181, 182
  preparation for, 23, 57
  results, 10-12, 19, 21, 23, 93
  strengthening, 185
  types, 17-18, 59-60, 64, 66
  with Plan, 94
World Teacher, 62-63
Christ-consciousness —
  achievement by humanity, 82, 158
  definition, 75
  embodiment, 75-76
  growth, stimulation, 83
  nurturing, in human heart, 47
  uprising, 48
Christ principle —
  in mankind, 36
  stimulation, 136
Christ within —
  control of individual life, 135-136
  evocation, 59
  power of, use, 131
  See also Christ-consciousness.
Christian, average, inertia, 166
Christianity —
  definition, 140
  emphasis upon immortality, 146
  errors, 63-64, 106
Christs, two, identity, 54
Church —
  authoritarianism, 164-165
  Christian, futility, 41-42, 63-64,
    80-81
  of Christ, true, 108
  situation today, 140
Churches —
  doom, 140
  Eastern, overemphasis, 144, 146
  housecleaning, 163
  outward show, 141-142
  revival in new form, 122
  Western, presentations, 144,
    146-147, 149-150
Churchianity —
  situation today, 17
  vulnerability, 140
Citizenship, world, training, 175
Civilisation —
  definition, 129
  new, attainment, 112
  present, death, 22-23
  quality and gifts to posterity,
    significance, 129
Conferences, cycle, 21, 22, 23
Consciousness —
  Christ. *See* Christ-consciousness
  expansion due to
    Reappearance, 153
  expansion in Christ, 25-27
  group, of Christ, 68-69
  group, stimulation, 21
  human —
    development, 12, 17-18
    expansion, 18
    five stages, 126
    new concepts, work with, 184
  initiate, concern, 27
  of disciples, stimulation, 86
  sentient area, nature and control,
    130-131
  spiritual, in man, stimulation by
    Christ, 47-48
Courage, need in raising money, 171
Cowardice, spiritual, 168
Creation, goal as love, 12
Crises of Christ. *See* Christ, crises.
Crisis —
  cyclic, in life on Earth, 57-58
  of Crucifixion, 53
Crucifixion —
  of Christ, symbolism, 97-98
  of Christ, triumph of, 52-53
  true meaning, 23

INDEX

Crystallisation, disruption, 18
Culture —
  esoteric relationship, 129
  production, relation to initiates, 129
Cycle of Conferences, significance, 21, 22, 23

D

Death, misconceptions, abolition, 123
Delusion, great, definition, 130
Democracy —
  present status, 164
  true, pre-requisites, 18
Desire —
  misuse, results, 20, 106, 132
  personal, energies, superseding, 131
Destruction by strengthened life in form, 94
Disciples —
  aid to Christ, 57
  entrance into Kingdom of Heaven, 100
  groups, attractive power, 72
  of Christ —
    announcement to, regarding decision, 30
    approach, 44
    attitude in service, 182
    belief in, 19
    Custodians of Mysteries, 123
    group, divisions, 183-184
    guidance, 43
    message today, 112
    presence, result, 128
    problem during World War, 90
    task, 67
    work with Plan, 94
  of Masters —
    love-wisdom expression, 92
    transmission of Forces of Restoration, 91
  preparation of humanity for Appearance, 84
  senior, training of beginners, 87
  spiritual tension, 73
  transfigured, expression of Light and Love, 134
  world —
    destruction of illusion and glamour, 133
    overshadowing by Christ, 48
Dispenser of Water of Life, 80, 83
Divine guidance, factual evidence, prophecy, 46-47
Divinity, communication with humanity, 6, 7, 10
Dualities, fused, demonstration, 98

E

Easter Festival, 155
Ecclesiasticism, freedom from, 17
Economic affairs, principle of sharing, 163
Education —
  new world, energies initiating, 91-92
  right, for Reappearance, 175
  world-wide, 18
Electricity, mystery, key, 123
Emotional —
  approach of religion, 158
  nature, characteristics and control, 130
Emotions, activity, effect of activation of heart, 135
Energies —
  new, needed and inflow, 85-86
  of enlightenment, 91-92
  planetary, uncontrolled, 123
Energy —
  and life, 89-90
  Aquarian, fusion with Piscean, 98
  direction, capacity, 94
  distributors, 89
  divine, transmission, 6
  extra-planetary, channel, 75
  generation and holding for future use, 73
  magnetic, vortex, 11
  of life, purpose and intention, 26
  of love and will, 62
  of will, distribution, 96
  Piscean, fusion with Aquarian, 98
  release by Christ, 88-95
Enlightenment, energies, 91-92
Error, discloser, 130
Esotericists, work, 19
Evil forces, entrenched, rout before coming of Christ, 163

Evocation —
  guarantee, 152
  use, 151
Evolution —
  demonstrations, 102-108
  development of Christ, 70
  nature of, 146
  of will, 71

F

Faiths, fusion, 158, 159
Fanaticism in religion today, 138, 141, 142
Fear —
  antidote, 187
  cultivation by churchmen, 142, 147
Festivals, religious —
  significance, 46
  world-wide, establishment, 154
  world-wide, nature of, 154-157
Financial —
  responsibility, lack, 173-175
  trusteeship, problem, 171
Fishes, astrological sign. See Piscean; Pisces.
Forces of Restoration, work, 90-92
Forms, all, God within, 150
Forums, enlightenment, 91-92
Four Noble Truths, 20, 106-107, 132, 133
France, maintenance of state of unrest, 176
Free will —
  expression, 113, 164
  sanctity, 164
Freedom —
  concepts brought by Hierarchy, 149
  conquest of tyranny, 164
  embodiment, 21
Frustration, sense, widespread, offsetting, 165
Full moon —
  Festivals, three, in 1945, 93
  of April, 1945, 90-91
  of June, 1945, 31, 75, 82, 86, 93
  of May, 1945, 91-92
Fusion —
  faiths, 158, 159
  goodwill, 186

  love and wisdom, 98, 101
  soul and personality, 134
  united aspiration to reach spiritual Hierarchy, 189
  will-to-good, 98, 123
Futility —
  individual, sense of, offsetting, 165
  of Christian Church, 41-42, 63-64, 80-81

G

Gemini Age, work of Masonic Fraternity, 126-127
Gethsemane experience, 28-29, 70, 97-98, 114
Glamour —
  dissipation —
    by Buddha, 132-135
    by Christ, 18, 131-135
    by man, 130-131, 132, 134-136
  plane, 130
  world, control, 131-133
  world, three aspects, 131
God —
  fact of, recognition, 144-145
  Heart, attunement with, 135
  idea of, types, 144-145
  immanent and transcendent, 12, 36, 37, 41, 144-145, 149-150
  Kingdom. See Kingdom of God.
  knowers, group potency, 182-183
  knowledge, revelation, 94
  love —
    agent, 87
    faith in, restoration, 19
    nature of, 131
    Principle, 12
    Revealers, 94, 148
  nature of, 113
  plans, manifestation, 157
  purpose, invocation, 157
  relationship of man to, 145
  representatives, 7, 10
  son, rightly functioning, 147
  Sons, manifestation, 169-170
  Spirit, work, 43
  will —
    agent, 87
    ascertained, 170
    implementation and

INDEX

manifestation, 157
or purpose, 13
ood, true, and beautiful —
 approach, 179
 responsibility for, 179-180
oodwill —
 development, result, 189
 era, inauguration, 112
 expression, 75, 84
 Festival, meaning, 155-156
 growth and spread, money for, 177-178, 179
 growth, expression, 164
 human, result, 40
 in men, 14
 men of —
  establishment of right human relations, 179
  first effort, 165
  individual workers in touch with, 171
  right action, importance, 39
  union, 21, 186
  work, 95, 112
 promotion by groups, 111
 spread and fusion into united working potency, 186
 transformation, 53
ospel story —
 nature of, 126
 study, 24-30
overnment, attention of Christ, 18
reat Britain, training of world, 175
reat White Lodge. *See* Hierarchy, Spiritual.
roup —
 Avatar, effect, 182-183
 consciousness, attainment, 119-120
 purpose, 72
 sentiency, expression, 131
 spirit, stimulation, 21
 will, mergence, 71
 work —
  of Aquarian Age, 182
  of Avatar of Synthesis, 77-78
  of Christ, 51
  spiritual, 48
roups —
 aid to New Group of World Servers, 111

 for production of right human relations, 111
 for promotion of goodwill, future, 111
 incarnation, 119
 invocative appeal, 22
 of disciples, transmission of Forces of Restoration, 91
 of energies ready for distribution, 95

H

Happiness, production and handling, 115
Hate —
 balance by goodwill, 74-75
 nature of, 112
Heart, magnetic qualities awakening, 128
Hearts of men, activation, effect on emotional activity, 135
Hell, doctrine, rejection, 146-147
Hercules —
 teaching, 103-104, 107
 twelve labours, 27
Hermes —
 quotation, 58
 teaching, 104
Hierarchy, Spiritual —
 advent, result, 130
 affairs, guidance, 43
 agency of Avatar of Synthesis, 78
 aid to —
  by humanitarians, 171
  Christ, 66
  humanity, 40
 anchorage, 78
 approach to humanity, 69, 148, 149
 at-one-ment with humanity, 153
 attitude in service, 182
 attractive power, 72
 communication with humanity, establishment, 151
 contact with Shamballa, 135
 critical activity, 169-170
 efforts, obstruction, 90
 emergence with Christ, 121
 entrance, 85
 externalisation, 169
 guarantee of Christ's coming, 49

guidance unrecognized, 184
Head, 29
initiation, 72
intensification of Light, 58
invocation, 157
knowledge regarding, 19
light, 34
main object, 93
nature of, 28
personnel, 59
problem, 102-103
readiness for coming of Christ, 38
respect for free will, 164
revelation of will-to-good and
  divine purpose, 77
Revelators, messages, 102-108
rhythm of life, 169
service of, 168
"standing", 95
stimulation of men, results, 129
synonyms, 148
transmission of Forces of
  Restoration, 91
visible presence, 123
work, 13, 18, 57, 93
History —
  future presentations, 129
  of mankind, nature of, 148
Holy days, universality in future, 154
Human —
  relations. See Right Human
    Relations.
  welfare and liberation, study, 21
Humanity —
  achievement of greater things than
    Christ, 107
  accomplishments to be aided by
    Christ, 49-53
  aid from Avatar of Synthesis and
    Christ, 93-94
  aid to divine Plan, 34-35
  belief in, need, 179
  condition, cause of Christ's
    emergence, 100
  decision, 72
  demand for light and contact with
    God, 148
  demand, united, result, 9, 10, 18
  destiny, spiritual, guardian, 43

disillusionment, 133
divine will for, 113
divinity, essential, belief in, 165
effort, goal, 132
emergence from dying
  civilisation, 22-23
enlightenment and loving
  activity, 134
expansions of consciousness, 127
hearts, attunement with Heart of
  God, 135
history, turning point, 135
invocation, results, 40, 43
invocative cry today, 42
lesson, 127
matured, realisation and loving
  activity, 134
maturity, approach, 135
mentally polarised, 158
misery, causes, 20, 106-107,
  113, 132
new concepts, work with, 184
needs, 11, 141-143
new race, 132
oneness, recognition, 78
opportunity today, 42
readiness for coming
  revelation, 133
recognitions, 41, 44
regeneration, 111
release into calm and freedom, 74
resurrection from materialism, 101
situation today, 30, 170
soundness today, 76
synthesis, 78
urge to betterment, 77
See also Man; Mankind.

I

Ideas, new, incoming, focus and
  release, 133
Identification with divine intention
  of Lord of World, 26
Illumination of personality, 134
Illusion, dissipation by Christ, 18,
  131, 132, 133
Illusions, creation, 131
Imam Mahdi, return, 5
Immortality —
  doctrine, importance, 147

INDEX

fact, recognition, 145-147, 150
proof, 105
teaching, 104-105
treatment by Christian
  Church, 146
Incarnation —
  motivation and direction, 119
  See also Law of Rebirth;
  Reincarnation.
India, group of thinkers, 105
Inertia —
  creeping, cure, 168
  of spiritual man, 166-171
Initiate, definition, 128
Initiates —
  cooperation with Christ, 69
  destruction of illusion and
    glamour, 133
  gathering by Christ and
    Buddha, 135
  source of culture, 129
  work, 13
Initiation —
  ascension, 54
  definition, 128
  first, 86, 87, 156
  hierarchical, 72
  Mysteries, restoration, 71
  Mysteries, revelation, 120-130
  of humanity, 82
  preparation for, 86
  second, 86
Initiations of Christ, 39, 54, 55
Inspiration, spiritual and ideational,
  work, 184
Intellect, unfolding, in religion,
  139-140
Intelligence of masses, stimulation, 91
Intelligentsia, awakening to
  recognition of humanity, 184-185
Intention, focussed willed, 94
International cooperation, 50, 59
Intuition of members of
  Hierarchy, 59
Intuitive —
  knowledge, foundation for faith
    and zeal, 187
  love, liberation by Christ, 111-112
  perception present today, 34
  perception, unfoldment in
    humanity, 88
  recognition of reality, 133
  research to meet challenge of
    Reappearance, 160
  understanding of Plan, 94
  understanding, pure expression, 97
Intuitives, world, new ideas, 133
Invocation —
  by —
    Christ, 46
    groups, 22
    humanity, 13, 40, 42, 43, 44
    trained disciples focussing cry of
      untrained, 152
  focussed, guarantee of
    evocation, 152
  Great, use, 31-35, 46, 72-73, 77, 82
  kinds, 151-152
  of Christ 22
  relation to power of thought, 154
  since 1935, results, 44-45
  spirit of worship and prayer,
    151-152
  telepathic activity, 154
  use, 151
  wordless cry of humanity, 151
Israel, children of, sin in desert,
  79, 81

J

Jerusalem, definition, 28, 57
Jesus —
  initiations, 39, 40
  overshadowing by Christ, 74
Jewish dispensation, 81, 106, 127, 145
Joy —
  in service, 168
  true, meaning, 115
June —
  Festival, 46, 155-156
  impact of energy, 75
  1945, work initiated, 93

K

Karma, re-emphasising, need for, 147
Kingdom of God —
  admission, 88, 159
  appearance, 120-121
  characteristics, 30
  citizens, 50-57, 65

definition, 50, 148
energies, 73
establishment, 65
expression of will-to-good, 77
laws governing Shamballa, 88
light, love, and power,
   channel, 186
manifestation, 65
materialisation, 71, 153
members, 126
mystical approach, 88
new world order, 169
orientation to, 119
public recognition, 163
right relation to era, 83
Knowledge, transmutation, 97
Krishna —
   cycle, 127
   reincarnation, prophecy, 4
   teaching, 107

L

Last Supper, symbolism, 80
Law of —
   Action and Reaction, wielding, 74
   Cause and Effect —
      reemphasising, need for, 147
      relation to evolution, 146
      relation to Law of Rebirth, 118
      salvation under, 147
   Compassion, result, 10
   Love, application, 132
   Rebirth —
      Eastern attitude, 115
      emphasis by Christ, 116
      misrepresentations, 117-118
      recognition, importance, 116, 120
      relation to evolution, 146
      relation to Law of
         Evolution, 115
      salvation under, 147
      teaching by Christ, 115-120
   Synthesis, demonstration, 77
Liberation —
   life of, key, 107-108
   Messenger of, 21
Life —
   Aspect, expression, 85
   more abundantly, definition,
      85, 112

more abundantly, goal, 146
new, tide, 95
Light —
   body full of, meaning, 134
   lines, establishment between
      groups, 59
   love, and service, unfolding realms,
      functioning in, 128
   of reason, destruction of
      glamour, 133
   planetary, source, 58
Lighted Way, treading, 21
"Little Ones", definition, 87
Lives, planetary, relationships, 153
Livingness —
   experiencing, result, 128
   interpretation, 85, 112-113
Lord of —
   Light. *See* Buddha, Lord.
   Love. *See* Christ.
   the World —
      aid to humanity, 44-45
      consultation with, 69
      intention, identification with, 26
      permission to use Invocation, 73
      presence, 46
      will, 13
      word or voice, 39, 40
Love —
   demonstration, prophecy, 75
   divine energy, transmission, 6
   embodiment, 34
   fusion with will-to-good, 98
   fusion with wisdom, 98, 101
   intuitive, released by Christ,
      results, 111-112
   light, and service, unfolding
      realms, functioning in, 128
   magnetic potency, 62
   of Christ, 9, 12, 36-37, 97
   of God —
      demonstration by Christ, 113
      faith in, restoration, 19
      nature of, 131
   Principle, transmission, 12
Love-wisdom energies, channeling
   to humanity, 92

M

Maitreya, return, 5

INDEX

Man, relationship to God, 145
Mankind —
  history, nature of, 148
  spiritual history, summary, 40-41
  See also Humanity.
Masonry —
  definition, 128
  failure, 124
  preservation of Mysteries, 121, 122
  two pillars, 126-127
Masters of the Wisdom —
  assistance to Christ, 51
  belief in, 19
  centre, 148
  communication with, 57
  cooperation with Christ, 69, 73
  disciples of Christ, 92
  existence as fact, 33
  existence, awareness of, 126
  groups of disciples, 72, 91
  love-wisdom, 92
  physical appearance, 121
  transmission of Forces of
    Restoration, 91
Materialism —
  in religion today, 140, 141
  rejection, 129
Matter, thralldom, release of
  humanity from, 134
May —
  1936, impact of Spirit of Peace, 75
  1945, full moon, 91-92
Messengers —
  from divine centre, constant
    emergence, fact, 150
  See also Avatar.
Messiah, Jewish, 81
Messiahs, doctrine, 6
Mind —
  agency in rebirth, 119
  discriminating faculty, 130
  divine, intention, perception, 70
  divine, penetration by searchlight
    of human mind, 128
  fused with will-to-good, 123
Minds of men, awakening, 91
Mithra —
  work, 127
  worship by Children of Israel,
    79, 81

Monadic realisation in Christ, 27-30
Money —
  channels of expenditure, 172-173
  deflection into channels of
    usefulness, 175-180
  for work of preparation for
    Christ, 166, 171-176
  misuse, 173-174
  use for Spiritual Hierarchy, era of,
    inauguration, 180
Moon, full, religious festivals, 154,
  155-156
Motherhood, instinctual,
  expression, 131
Moving picture, enlightenment, 91-92
Mysteries —
  ancient —
    content, 122, 123
    origin, 122
  restoration, 121, 122
  of initiation, 71, 125
  of Mithras, 127
  relation to electricity, 123
  sequence, 126-127
  source of revelation, 123
Mystic, new type, 33-34

N

New Age —
  Builder, 98
  humanity, 158
  inauguration, aid, objective,
    188-189
  introduction, 78
  prophecies, 22-23, 33, 101
  religion. *See* Religion, new world.
  ushering in, 182
New Group of World Servers —
  aid by groups, 111
  aid to Avatar of Synthesis, 77-78
  first effort, 165
  functions, 78
  invocation by, 151
  Leader, 46
  major objective, 78
  overshadowing by Christ, 48
  personnel, 183-184, 186
  position, 166
  readiness, 95
  recognition, 185

INDEX

success, 185-186
susceptibility to energies of
  enlightenment, 92
tasks, 185, 186
telepathic activity, 154
training and mission, 100
work, 44, 84, 90, 98, 114, 181,
  184, 185
New Life, tide, 95
New Testament —
  astrological teaching, 79
  story, 100
Newspaper men, enlightenment with
  new ideas, 92
Noble Eightfold Path, 20-21
Noble Middle Way, 90
Nourisher of the Little Ones, 83, 86

O

Occultists, work, 19
Old Testament, astrological
  teaching, 79
Overshadowing of —
  Christ by Spirit of Peace, 74-75
  disciples by Christ, 48
  Jesus by Christ, 74

P

Path —
  of Discipleship, seeking, 168
  of Evolution, nature of, 146
  of Evolution, step forward, 61
  to God, existence, knowledge
    of 150
Peace —
  attainment, 14, 40, 41
  basis, 59, 149
  on earth, era, inauguration, 112
  restoration before coming of
    Christ, 163
Personality —
  integrated, of disciple, 134
  purified, dedicated, and
    illumined, 134
Piscean Age —
  demands, 182
  end, 123
  influence, 81, 106
  Teacher, 79
  unfoldment of humanity, 84

work of Christ, 88, 98, 99
Plan —
  aid by humanity, 34-35
  divine, manifestation, 65
  for world, guarantee, 145
  knowledge of by Christ, 25, 26
  motivation, 12
  readiness, 95
  understanding, 46, 94
Plane —
  astral, definition, 130
  astral, work of Buddha, 134-135
  mental, work of Christ, 135
  physical, spiritual importance, 178
Point within the Triangle, 83, 84
Political —
  groups, house-cleaning before
    coming of Christ, 163
  system, authoritarianism, 164-165
Politics, divorce from religion,
  cessation, 18-19
Power, storehouse and use, 73
Prayer —
  answers, 35
  substitution for, 151
  to God Transcendent, 32-33
Press, enlightenment, 92
Principle of directed Purpose, 94
Prophecies regarding —
  Aquarian Age, 129
  attitude toward Christ, 66
  authoritarianism, 164-165
  Buddha's work, 93, 96-97
  Christ's coming, publicity, 16-17
  Christ's future names, 83
  Christ's teaching, 23, 115-130
  Christ's work, 88, 96, 122-123, 124,
    125, 135
  churches, 140
  distribution of energy of love,
    111-113
  factual evidence of divine
    guidance, 46-47
  goodwill, 84
  group work, 182
  Hierarchy, 153
  history, 129
  holy days, 154
  initiation, 86
  invocation, 151, 152

INDEX

kingdoms of nature, 78
materialism, 129
Mysteries, 122-123
New Age, 22-23, 33, 101
new world religion, 149-151, 152, 159
peace, 40, 41
psychic powers, 123
reincarnation of Krishna, 4
religious Festivals, 155-157
representatives of God, 7
restoration of true religion, 17
right human relations, 84, 111-112, 113
science of invocation and evocation, 151
spread of true teaching, 140
study of Christ's work, 66
United Nations, 50
Psychic powers, future use, 123
Publishers of world literature, enlightenment, 92
Purpose, divine —
  demonstration, 113
  for earth life, 145

Q

Questions —
  in India, 105
  religion, 138-139

R

Radio, enlightenment, 91-92
Ram, astrological sign. See Aries.
Reactionary forces in every nation, arrest, results, 188-189
Reality —
  intuitive recognition, 133
  perception, lack in man, 103
  spiritual, focus of religious spirit, 137
Rebirth —
  Law. See Law of Rebirth.
  teaching by Christ, 115-120
Recognition, spiritual, development, 19
Recognitions, divine, training in, 59
Reconstruction, aid, means, 58-59
Reincarnation —
  meaning and teaching, 117
  of Krishna, prophecy, 4
  See also Incarnation; Law of Rebirth; Rebirth.
Religion —
  definitions, 43, 157-158
  divorce from politics, cessation, 18-19
  nature in past, 158
  new world —
    basic ceremony, 86
    basis, 71, 143-152, 157
    doctrine of rebirth, 116
    implementation, 159
    inauguration, 72, 83
    keynote, 82, 150, 152
    method, 151, 152
    platform, 158-159
    ritual, 153-154
    structure, 67
    theme, 150
    vision, 149
  organisation, failure, 138-139
  orthodox, situation today, 137-138
  outward show, 141-142
  technique in past, 158
  true, emergence, 42-43
  true, restoration, 17
Religions, world —
  failure, 124
  teaching underlying, concepts, 103, 113
Religious —
  faith, sectarian, unimportance, 60
  spirit fundamentally alive, 137
  spirit, growth, blocking, 142
Renunciation —
  of materialistic standards, 127
  true meaning, 23
Resurrection —
  life, message, 23
  of humanity, 23, 30
  period, inauguration, 23
Revelation —
  continuity, 9-10, 61, 62, 64 65, 147-148
  divine, factual nature, 64, 150
  divine worldwide, 62-63
  new, expectancy, 143, 149
  of divinity, twelve festivals, 157
  of truth, hindrance, 141

source, true, 123
spiritual, basis, 6
Right human relations —
  approach, 149
  attainment, means, 53, 75
  attainment, results, 112
  basis, 59
  beginning, 165
  demonstration, 21
  desire for, 46
  doctrine, preaching, 112
  due to developing spiritual attitude, 41
  era, beginning, 83
  establishment —
    agents, 95
    by disciples, 30-31
    by Hierarchy, 18, 30-31
    by humanity, teaching, 115
    by New Group of World Servers, 186
    expression of Christ-consciousness, 47
    factors involved, 115
    financial support, 172, 177, 178, 179
    major task of Christ, 56, 57
    mode, 107
    prevention by Christian Church, 12
    relation to divine will, 113
  evocation, 84
  expression, 155
  Light and life, 58
  need for and importance, 108-109
  need for, education in, 175
  new demands, 143
  program, 132
  promotion by groups, 111
  relation to doctrine of rebirth, 116
  requirement for coming of Christ, 12, 13, 188, 189
  results, 78, 96
  seekers, 110-111
  sign of approach of Christ, 44
  teaching of Buddha, 20
  with God, 20
  with humanity, 20
  with life in all forms, 120
Rudhyar, Dane: *New Mansions for New Men*, quotation, 117
Russia, desired handling of world finances, 175

S

Salvation —
  of world in hands of people, 162
  personal, concept, shift from, 171
  self-achieved, through reincarnation and karma, 147
Sankaracharya —
  cycle, 127
  teaching, 107
Saviour —
  coming, cause, 10
  expectancy, 5-6
  See also Avatar; Messengers; Teacher, world.
Saviours, world, source, 58
Scapegoat, teaching, 79, 81, 106
Science —
  of invocation and evocation —
    definition, 151
    functions, 152-153
    use, results, 153
  revelation of Mysteries, 122-123
Scriptures, world —
  common doctrine, 6
  prophecies, 45
  symbolism of narrative, 59
  writing, procedure, 154
Self-sacrifice, need in raising money, 177-178
Service —
  joy in, 168
  light, and love, unfolding realms, functioning in, 128
  of individual in work of preparation, 180-181
  technique, teaching, 107-108
Shamballa —
  aid to Avatar of Synthesis, 78
  centre, orientation, to, 28
  contact with Hierarchy, 135
  fiat for the Reappearance, 39
  impact of human vibration, 158
  Intermediary with Hierarchy, 155
  laws governing, 88
  spread of Light, 58

INDEX

Sharing —
    Aquarian, 80, 82
    principle, control of economic affairs, 163
    principle, growth, 76
Sin against Holy Ghost, 112
Social workers, enlightenment, 92
Sons of —
    God, manifestation, 169-170
    God, teachings, 102-108
    man, radiation and response to light, 13-14
Sorrow, cause, 20, 106, 113, 132
Soul —
    attractive power becoming dominant, 71-72
    definition, 124
    factual existence, establishment, 123-124
    factual nature, recognition, 105
    famine, 143
    human pilgrimage, 159
    intermediation, 6
    light on Way, 34
    nature of, 134
    reincarnation, 118-119
    will aspect, expression, 118
Souls in concerted action, 9
Spirit of Peace —
    descent upon Christ, 74
    work, 74-75, 82, 101, 111
Spiritual —
    cowardice, 168
    Hierarchy. *See* Hierarchy, Spiritual.
    life in circumstances and environment, 167-168
    life, unfoldment, hindrance, 141
    living, restoration, 17
    man, inertia, 166-171
    recognition, 19
    resources, pooling, 154-157
    understanding, growth, 164
Spiritualistic movement, work, present, 104
Spiritualists, work, 19-20
St. Paul, influence, 106, 140
Subhuman kingdoms, right relations with humanity, 78

Synthesis —
    human, production, 78
    in spiritual fellowship, 158
    See also Avatar of Synthesis.

T

Tabernacle in the wilderness, symbolism, 28
Taurus, Age —
    world Teacher, 127
    worship, 79, 81, 106
Teacher, World, 62-63, 86
Teachers, World, source, 58
Telepathic activity in invocation, 154
Temple of Solomon, symbolism, 27-28
Tension —
    emotional, today, effect on humanity, 135
    point, definition, 73
    spiritual, work of preparation, 73
Theologians, formulations, 137-138, 140, 141, 142
Thinkers, world, new ideas, 133
Thought power, relation to invocation, 154
Thoughtform, potent, of Avatar, 11
Training, esoteric or spiritual, 99
Transfiguration —
    interpretation, 51-52
    meaning, 134
Transmigration, confusion with reincarnation, 115-116
Transmutation of knowledge, 18, 97
Triangle, Buddha-Spirit of Peace-Avatar of Synthesis, 111
Truth —
    divine, presentation, failure, cause, 139-140
    divine, recognition by man, aid, 103
    dynamic, anchorage, 11
    of immanence of God, proof, 149-150
    recognition, causal process, 134
    religious, presentation, 142
    revealer, 130
    revelation, new, search for, 138
Truths —
    distinctive of Christ, Buddha, and

Church of God, 66
new, 12, 36, 48, 53
Twelve, symbolism, 27

U

Understanding —
  blossoming, prophecy, 14
  intuitive. *See* Intuitive understanding.
  loving, international, 132
  new era, inauguration, 188
  of Plan, 94
  spiritual, growth, 164
United Nations —
  Assembly, work of Hierarchy, 93
  need, 132
  prophecy, 50
  rapacious demands, 174-175
  work of Avatar of Synthesis, 77
United States —
  imposition of democracy upon world, 175-176
  selfishness, 128

V

Vicarious atonement, doctrine, 106
Vyasa, teaching, 104-105, 107

W

War —
  cause, 113
  World, results, 42
Water-Bearer, astrological sign. *See* Aquarian; Aquarius.
Water of Life, Dispenser, 83, 84-86
Way —
  Lighted, definition, 30
  of —
    Resurrection, 30
    the Heart, combination with Way of the Mind, 93
    the Higher Evolution, 26
    the Mind, combination with Way of the Heart, 93
Welfare work, trend, 22
Wesak Festival —
  meaning, 155
  participation of Buddha, 96
  purpose, 45-46

Will —
  Aspect. *See* Aspect, will.
  divine —
    anchorage, 53
    dynamic effectiveness, 62
    for humanity, 113
    interpretation, 71
    submission to, 114, 115
  energy, distribution, 96
  evolution of, 71
  group, mergence, 71
  in focussed intention, 94
  of Christ, 29-30, 70, 73, 76-77
  of God, 13, 31, 34, 62, 69, 71, 87, 113
  potency, awareness of, 27
  use in transfiguration of lower nature, 30
  See also Free will.
Will-to-good —
  activities today, 169
  expression, 173
  flowering, 14
  fused with mind, 123
  fusion with Love, 98
  generation in humanity, 77
  transformations, 40, 53, 57
Will-to-unity, generation, 77
Wine, symbolism, 80
Wisdom —
  from knowledge, 97
  fusion with love, 98, 101
  of Buddha, 134
  of Christ, 97
Words, formulas, use in invocative work, 152
Worker, individual, requirements for service of Christ, 180-181
World —
  order, new, 132, 169
  situation today, 15-35
Worlds of meaning and experience, blending, 129-130
Worship, substitution for, 151
Writers, enlightenment, 92

Y

Youth, revolt in religion, 138